Worcester's Union Station

The Monument and the Memories

Idamay Michaud Arsenault

TO: SUSAN

FROM:

Idamay

Ambassador Books • Worcester, Massachusetts

ISBN: 0-9646439-1-X
Library of Congress Catalog Card Number: 99-068270

Published in the United States by Ambassador Books, Inc.
71 Elm Street, Worcester, Massachusetts 01609
(800) 577-0909

Printed in Canada.

For current information about all titles from Ambassador Books, visit our website at:
www.ambassadorbooks.com

In memory of my parents,
Gabriel and Anna (LeBrasseur) Michaud
who set the foundation
for my love of reading, writing, and 'bonne humeur,'
and to the educators who molded my thoughts
from kindergarten through college.

Throughout our history, Worcester has been a City of great diversity. We are a City of immigrants. Worcester is a place where people, who can trace their heritage to virtually every country on the face of the earth, are welcomed members of our community.

Union Station is an important part of our City's history. More than just a majestic building, Union Station has served as a welcoming "port of entry" for many immigrants who came to Worcester looking to start a new life. Over the years, as wave after wave of new immigrant groups arrived, Union Station became a symbol of our immigrant heritage.

Today, as we rebuild this wonderful link to our past, Worcester's citizens are reminded of their own family's story and the vital role that immigrants played in the building of our community. It is a story worth remembering.

Sincerely,

Raymond V. Mariano

Mayor, City of Worcester

CONTENTS

ACKNOWLEDGEMENTS

My grateful appreciation to:

Dr. Claire Quintal, Founding Directress Emerita of the French Institute at Assumption College, Worcester, for suggesting helpful books for the French Connection chapter of this book.

Julie Sanders, former Project manager and architect for the Union Station Restoration Project at Worcester Redevelopment Authority, who allowed me to take photos of the interior of Union Station, and accompanied me time and again when crossing Washington Square.

James Igoe, Executive Director of Preservation Worcester (PW) and to his assistant, Marilynn Borst, for their friendship; permission to do research in PW's archives, and for their interest and support throughout the project.

Carolyn C. Hallin, Director, RSVP (Retired and Senior Volunteer Program) Worcester, whose newsletter led me to several interesting interviewees, and for her keen interest and support.

Peter Faulkner, photography teacher at the Worcester Center for Crafts for putting up with me, and for his interest in my work while attending classes there.

Betty Jenewin, photographer at the Worcester Telegram & Gazette, whose front page photo of the interior of Union Station inspired me to shoot more photos of the station, and for connecting me with Julie Sanders at WRA.

Gerard E. Goggins, President, publisher and editor of Ambassador Books, Inc., of Worcester, for his guidance, encouragement, and helpful suggestions.

Jennifer A. Goggins, for her painstaking work and skills at editing and revisions.

Sister Susan Terkanian, S.S.A., for her ideas in layout and design.

Mayor Raymond V. Mariano, for his interesting contribution and insight for the future of Union Station.

Nancy Gaudette, Worcester Room, at the Worcester Public Library, for finding information when I had no clue where to look.

John Riccio, Assistant Principal at Clark Street School, Worcester, for his tireless efforts to track down some students and teachers who traveled from Union Station to Hartford, CT. in 1974.

Margaret A. Erskine, Worcester historian, for permission to print excerpts from her book, *Heart of the Commonwealth-Worcester*.

John McDevitt, Publisher, Jemtech Digital Publishing, Cumberland, RI. for permission to adapt from the book, *Heritage of Peace, Land of Hope and Glory*, by Corinne Rocheleau Rouleau of Worcester, and Louise Lind of Greenville, RI.

Zabelle D'Amico, talk show host on Holden cable television, for exposure of my photographs of Union Station, and for promoting my book on her Faces and Places program.

Mimi Grenier, Director of Exhibits at the Worcester Public Library, for exhibiting 52 photographs of Union Station in January/February, 1998.

Marcel Raymond, host of L'Heure Francaise radio program, for planning speaking engagements about my book and photographs.

Theresa B. Davitt, Librarian at the Worcester Historical Museum for assisting me in my quest for unique photos from the turn of the century.

Worcester Telegram & Gazette library personnel for their permission to print text and photos from their files.

Gloria Woodman, and Pat Fisher, friends and fellow photographers, who were always there to help hang my Union Station exhibits.

William W. Mackin, construction manager of Union Station, for his willingness to accommodate me when taking new shots of the station.

Michael W. Coonan, newly elected labor representative at WRA who put in a good word for me at his first board meeting.

My daughter Denise Hobby, for assisting me in the arduous task of taking the final shots of the interior and exterior of the station on flag testing day.

My brother, Oscar J. Michaud for digging up old photos and memories of our past that were fitting for this book.

Lastly, the wonderful individuals I interviewed without whom this book would not have been possible.

—A very special thank you to —
my husband, Jerry,
who spent many nights watching "Home Improvement" reruns by himself, and for buying me all the 'toys' I needed (computer, printer, scanner, copier) to facilitate the writing of this book.

Our yesterdays follow us,
they constitute our life,
and they give character and force and meaning
to our present deeds.

— Joseph Parker —

Chapter One

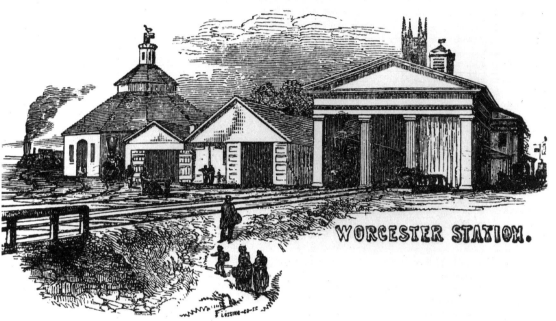

An artist's sketch of Worcester's first railroad station.

Early Times

Long before Europeans landed on America's shores, Indian tribes inhabited an area near what is now called Lake Quinsigamond in Worcester, Massachusetts. The Indians had no horses, wagons, or carts. Their only mode of land travel was by foot. Indian tribes settled near bodies of water to enable them to fish, build canoes, and navigate the waterways. They remained until they were driven out by the Europeans.

A settlement called Quinsigamond Plantation was established on the site of present day Worcester in 1673, but it was abandoned two years later. In 1684, it was resettled and named Worcester. In 1702, it was abandoned again, but it was permanently settled in 1722, and chartered as a City in 1848.

In the eighteenth century, getting from one place to another was a slow process. Horse-and-carriage travel was hampered by muddy streets and cobblestone roads. A physically fit person could run faster than the 'contraptions' could move. The wealthy rode in their own fancy carriages; while everyone else either rode in horse-drawn wagons or walked.

Life changed dramatically after Benjamin Wright engineered the Blackstone Canal in 1828. From Worcester to Providence, Rhode Island, factories sprung up along the banks of the Blackstone.

It was a time of change and growth. Major industrial development occurred causing a drastic change in the way things were produced. What had once been hand-crafted was now being machine-manufactured in factories. Inventions proliferated and changed forever the way people lived. According to the National Park Service, U.S. Department of the Interior, the Blackstone River Valley was the birthplace of the American Industrial Revolution, with the Blackstone Canal as the catalyst. However, with the advent of the railroad in 1832, the service of the canal was short-lived.

Worcester was affected by these changes, too. From 1830 to 1845, the population of the town quadrupled. This rapid expansion resulted in part by the introduction of railroads.

Worcester was first visited by locomotives in 1835. They chugged through the city at an incredible thirty miles an hour. The first locomotive arrived on July 4, 1835, and within a few years, six railroads were coming into Worcester.

To accommodate the growing number of rail travelers, the Boston Passenger House was built on Foster Street at Norwich Street. Also known as the Boston and Worcester Depot, the terminal opened in 1847.

The Boston and Worcester Depot was Worcester's primary rail depot. Huge throngs gathered to witness the arrival of the first steam engines with great excitement. Along with other nationalities, many French-

Courtesy of Gertrude Lacey

The Old Boston and Worcester Depot, Foster Street

Canadians bound for all parts of New England stopped at the station. A man named Cote acted as interpreter for these French people, and thus, among the French-Canadians, the Foster Street Depot was popularly known as Old Cote's Depot.

In little more than a quarter of a century, the depot could no longer handle the increasing traffic. This led to the construction of the first Union Station which was built in 1874-1875. Known as Union Passenger Station and later as Old Union Station, the station formally opened on June 1, 1875. It was located on the northwest corner of Washington Square on the site of Elliot Swan's Washington Square Hotel.

The Worcester Illustrated Business Guide, a publication printed by Railroad Printers during the 1800s, notes that the station was one of the most elegant structures of its kind in the United States. Designed by architects Ware and Van Brunt, the general architecture was gothic in style, and the station's two hundred foot Norman-style clock tower instantly became a focal point of the city.

Old Union Station was the Grand Central Station for all the railroads entering or passing through Worcester, which included the Boston & Albany, the Providence & Worcester, and the Norwich & Fitchburg. Most stages and omnibuses that ran to towns in the county arrived and departed from Old Union Station.

Old Union Station was designed to accommodate rail travel for at least a cen-

tury. But the popularity of rail travel increased drastically, and by 1898, 140 trains brought more than ten thousand passengers through Worcester daily. The station could not handle the high volume. In addition, grade crossings, trolley tracks, and intersecting roads became a serious problem.

By the early twentieth century, the ground-level tracks of Old Union Station required replacement, and it became necessary to elevate in-town railroad tracks. At the same time, textile mills were growing in number and businesses were thriving in the area. The combination of these factors warranted the construction of a new Union Station.

Courtesy of Gertrude Lacey

Elliot Swan's Hotel on the site of the 1875 Union Station.

13

The first Union Station.

An E.B. Luce photo courtesy of Yvonne LaPointe

In 1909, construction began on the present Union Station located on the northeast corner of Washington Square. However, work on the station was delayed by the close proximity of the Blackstone Canal bed — which, at the time, was used as a sewer. Special engineering was required for the support of the foundation, and construction was completed in 1911.

A Preservation Worcester Newsletter relates that upon its opening in 1911, the new Union Station was hailed as one of the grandest in the nation. Designed by Watson & Huckel of Philadelphia, Pennsylvania, it was modeled after a Roman basilica. Its design is French Renaissance, intermingled with Greek Art, and lace-like ornamentation of the Orient.

During the early twentieth century the station was an object of civic pride for its vast scale, elaborate classical design and heavy train traffic. It was known as the city's most imposing example of Beaux Arts Classical architecture, one which also served as a major local landmark by virtue of its grand scale and prominent site. Construction costs were $750,000 and were part of a three million dollar project to eliminate grade crossings in the city. The ornate white terra cotta building was called the "Million Dollar Union Station."

The train tracks had been elevated on stone embankments which had subway passages that led into the building. In 1914, one hundred trains stopped at Union Station daily. During its major period of activity, Union Station served the Boston & Albany, the Boston & Maine, the New York & New Haven and the New York Central Railroad companies.

The new station had all the conveniences known at the time. There were freight elevators for mail and baggage, a "Ladies Cafe" and a gentlemen's "Smoking Room." The first floor was used as a large waiting room, while the second floor housed railroad offices, mail, and offices for various freight companies. A special driveway led to the front entrance for the use of passengers arriving by coach or cab. There were once five barbers employed in Charley Podbielski's Union Station barber shop.

The new Union Station was intended to be the finest of its size in the country. The glass dome over the main waiting room was decorated with the state seal, and the main entries were framed by marble Ionic half-columns. The new edifice was described by American and European architects as one of the best and most unique in the country. Local publications called it "a poem in stone" and said it was "built to last".

Upon entering the front doors, there was the gentlemen's waiting room on the left, a well-arranged office in the center; and the ladies waiting room directly east on the same side. On the right of the main entrance were the baggage rooms, express package office, news office, telegraph and Station Master's rooms, and a large and well arranged dining room eighty feet long and forty-seven feet wide. These rooms were arranged on either side of a large vestibule and were open to the roof. Above these rooms were the offices of various railroads which were based in Worcester, and the private office of Henry P. Nichols, Esquire, the agent of the Boston and Albany railroad.

Passing through the vestibule, the patrons would enter into an immense double-arched enclosure where the passenger trains arrived and departed. The double roof was a remarkable iron structure. Each section had a span of 125 feet and was fifty feet in height. It was supported by eight wrought-iron trestles, which rested on cast iron columns eighteen inches in diameter and thirty feet high upon walls of the most substantial granite.

Worcester historian, Margaret A. Erskine, states in her book, *The Heart of the Commonwealth — Worcester.* (1985):

The slow decline of the passenger train began in the 1920s, with the rise of commercial aviation and the automobile. Planes were faster, and the auto allowed a greater sense of flexibility in traveling that a railroad schedule didn't.

During the years the station also had changed. The twin towers were removed in 1926 due to vibrations caused by the trains. The handsome canopies over the front entrance came down in 1941.

After World War II, automobiles, trucks, and buses replaced trains throughout the nation. In Worcester, the transition is symbolized by Washington Square, whose urban form was sacrificed to the elevated roadbed of I-290 and its attendant rotary in the 1950s.

Worcester Center Boulevard completed the job in ensuing decades by severing Washington Square's connections with City Hall and Main Street.

By the late 1950s, railroads sought to eliminate passenger service by reducing red ink and restructuring operations around their more profitable freight traffic.

The Interstate Highway Act, signed by President Eisenhower in 1956, hastened the decline of the passenger train. This act made a national network of high-speed interstate highways a reality and left passenger railroads to totter on the brink of extinction. The traveling public in ever-increasing numbers turned towards airplanes and the automobile to get from there to here.

From the 1870s to the late 1920s, Washington Square was a primary focal point of Worcester's streetcar system, according to Burton B. Shaw of Worcester.

A trolley car buff for many years, Shaw says that the design of Union Station and its location relative to the adjacent railroad tracks provided space for a trolley terminal under the bridge spanning Front Street. Trolley cars ran up and down Front Street and through Washington Square in front of the station. Directly under the railroad bridge, trolley tracks turned off the street into a sheltered area next to the station building. There were three bays which were formed by the bridge's support columns, and each bay had track long enough to hold at least two trolley cars. A small booth was located in the area for a dispatcher, or starter, whose duty it was to control trolley traffic. This terminal served some of the suburban and interurban trolley lines, such as Fitchburg, Marlboro, and Holden, as well as a few of the city lines, such as the Webster Square, Moore Avenue, and Lincoln Square lines.

The trolley routes changed from time to time depending on scheduling and the change in volume of passengers. Some routes were added to, others dropped from using the Union Station terminal. As time passed, an increasing number of trolley lines were converted to bus operation. Suburban service was drastically cut back, causing the Union Station trolley terminal to eventually close. The terminal at Salem Square serviced the few remaining suburban trolley lines.

It should be noted that The Boston and Worcester interurban line did not use the Union Station terminal, but came up Front Street into Salem Square.

*T*rolleys required a motorman to run the trolley and a conductor to collect fares. At one time, trolley car fare cost five cents, but when Shaw started using the service in the 1920s, the fare had increased to ten cents. He recalls getting on the trolley, putting a dime in the fare box, and getting a free transfer when he traveled farther than downtown.

During rush hours, cars were crowded and many passengers had to stand. Shaw's favorite place to stand was beside the motorman in the front vestibule, because from this vantage point, he could watch the motorman operate the controls.

At the end of the day, the cars were stored in car barns. One such barn was on Main Street at the corner of Market Street in the vicinity of Wesley Church near Lincoln Square, another on Main Street at the corner of Gates Lane, and another on Grove Street. The Gates Lane car barn was converted to a bus garage in the late 1930s.

Most of the city trolley lines traveled from one side of the city to the other, passing through the center of Worcester near Harrington Corner. For example, the Tatnuck line travelled down Pleasant Street, past City Hall, and up Grafton Street and Hamilton Street to the entrance of Lake Park.

At the time, Shaw lived on Flagg Street, off Pleasant Street. He recalls that in order to go to the YMCA (Young Men's Christian Association) on Main Street, he would take the car from Tatnuck and transfer at City Hall to the Burncoat car bound for Cherry Valley by way of Main Street.

During rush hours, extra cars were added to the heavier traveled routes, but they did not travel to the end of the lines. For instance, the extra cars on the Tatnuck and West Tatnuck lines would stop at either Moore Avenue or Tatnuck Square.

In the end, trolley cars went the way of the Conestoga wagon. The last few trolley lines used Market Street until the end of Worcester's trolley service on December 31, 1945.

Shaw never lost interest in trolley car history and memorabilia. He is the proud owner of a trolley car fare register which he bought at a flea market in Searsport, Maine, for about thirty-five dollars.

From May until September, Shaw can be found at the Seashore Trolley Museum in Kennebunkport, Maine where he works as an Instructor/Inspector. He uses his trolley expertise to teach new motormen how to operate the cars.

A long time volunteer at RSVP (Retired and Senior Volunteer Program), Shaw devotes one day a week at the Fairlawn Rehabilitation Hospital handling interoffice mail.

Burton Shaw

E.B. Luce Photo

Union Station with its original towers shortly after its construction.

18

E.B. Luce photo

Cars parked in front of the station in the 1930s.

The Union Passenger Station was busy from 1875 to 1911 — only thirty-four years. Its structure survived until January 1959. A Boston company bid ten thousand dollars to demolish it — and spent twenty-two thousand dollars getting the job done.

As for Union Station, the last passenger disembarked from a train at 9:23 P.M. on Saturday, October 24, 1964. His name is Philip C. Martin of Waterford, Connecticut. He was a senior at Worcester Polytechnic Institute. After 1964, the station remained vacant until it finally closed in 1972. By the mid-seventies, the building's exterior and interior had been largely destroyed.

Since 1964, there were many newspaper accounts of various groups attempting to buy the station. The impending fate of it seemed to change almost daily. Proposals to save the station came and went.

The building was proposed as the site for a police station in 1966. Renovation as a community theater was proposed in 1971. Worcester Center Associates considered buying the building the same year. The station finally closed in 1972. In 1973, a proposal was floated to use the building as a sports and convention center. The University of Massachusetts considered buying it for a medical school site.

19

In 1983, it was bought by Raymond LaRosa of Rye, New Hampshire, for $201,500. LaRosa planned a Quincy Market-style renovation, and then a forty-six million dollar Convention Center.

LaRosa sold the building in 1985 to Angelo Scola Jr., Frank Noel Jr., and Kevin Giblin. LaRosa's interest in the building became the focus of a federal racketeering investigation.

In subsequent years, it seemed there was no hope for the future of the station, until WRA (Worcester Redevelopment

E.B. Luce photo

Union Station in 1920 before the towers were removed.

E.B. Luce photo

Union Station after the twin towers were removed in 1926.

Authority) bought the building in the fall of 1994, with the intention of turning it into an intermodal transportation center. The firm of Finegold, Alexander & Associates of Boston in association with Harry Weese Associates of Washington, D.C. was selected as the Architectural/Engineering team for design of the project. *Some of the above information was taken from an article "Facts and Figures" published in the Telegram and Gazette on August 8, 1992. Used with permission.*

Vaulted windows without their stained glass in 1994.

Brian Mura Photo

The balcony in 1972.

An interior view of Union Station as reconstruction began in 1996.

I remember Union Station's vast interior with its shiny black benches and the giant locomotive that spewed steam like a fierce dragon as it started its journey.

Chapter Two

Childhood Recollections

Using the 48-step foot-bridge that connected Canterbury Street to Crystal and Illinois Streets was an adventure for the author and her siblings.

*A*h, Worcester! My kind of "town." It's been my kind of town since I was two years old. We arrived in the big city — all eleven of us — bag and baggage in a rundown truck and my brother Leo's old black Marmon touring car. We traveled from Southwick, Massachusetts, where my parents and older brothers and sisters worked on the tobacco farms. We rented a house on Mill Street for about a year then we moved to 207 Cambridge Street.

Before I was aware of Union Station in Worcester, I was fascinated by the trains that traveled near our house on the Boston and Albany railroad tracks. The black wooden forty-eight-step

bridge that spanned the tracks from Canterbury Street to Crystal and Illinois Streets was a daily trek for my sisters Angelina, Roseanna, and me to get to Holy Name of Jesus School.

We lived in a three-decker about two or three miles west of Union Station. It was a six-room, cold-water flat — meaning there was no central heating system. What in those days was called a "flat" or a "tenement" is referred to today as an "apartment." We had a cast-iron wood/coal stove that was later converted to an oil range. Two burners were fed by range oil from a green glass tank at the rear of the stove. When the bubbles "glooglooed" in the tank, Ma or Pa would strike a match to ignite the

Leo's Marmon touring car.

Our father made home-made bread, and our mother baked mouth-watering apple pies and the best molasses cookies ever made. In winter, the only warm room in our house was the kitchen. On cold mornings, it was a race to see who would get to the front of the stove first. When we got up, the stove had already been lighted by Ma or Pa, and whoever got to the kitchen first got the front spot. Most mornings, however, our Grandfather LeBrasseur was already there with his back to the oven, smoking his corn cob pipe. He would not budge, and we never objected. Our grandmother, who always got up before the birds, would already have made a pot of Orange Pekoe tea and would be sipping away in the rickety old rocker on the other side of the stove.

wicks. Water was heated in galvanized tubs for bathing, washing clothes, and washing dishes. Supper was prepared early in the morning and simmered on the stove all day. I guess whoever invented the crock-pot knew something about the slow cooking process that enhanced the flavor of food in "the olden days." Every meal was delicious. Our mother could make a chuck roast and a few vegetables look like a banquet.

The back of our house was on Canterbury Street just a few steps from the forty-eight-step bridge we crossed every school day and on Sundays to go to Mass. I counted the steps every day just because I thought it was fun. Twelve steps up, then a landing, twelve more steps up; across the bridge, then twelve steps down; another landing, and twelve more steps down until I got to the other side.

The families who lived on the Canterbury Street side of the tracks (us) I perceived as the poor people, and the families who lived on the Crystal/Illinois side of the tracks (they) were the rich people. It seemed that way to me because most of the kids who lived "over there" had better houses, nicer clothes, and (they) could afford the ten-cents a week tuition and one-dollar a week for piano lessons. Most of their fathers had cars and drove the nuns to where ever they needed to go, and (they) lived next to Crystal Park. We didn't even have a yard. We had a little patch of grass next to the cement steps in the front of the house where my sister Virginia took family photos with her Brownie Box camera.

Many times, my sisters and I would risk being late for class and stop in the middle of the bridge to watch an approaching train. The rumble of the train vibrated through the old wood-

The author (foreground) with sisters Roseanna (left) and Angelina, and their friend, Clifford Gordon.

en planks underfoot as we tight-ly held on to the wrought iron railing.

When I was eight, we moved to Salem Street, away from familiar sights, sounds, and smells. After the moving truck and Leo's Marmon touring car with our modest belongings left our old neighborhood, my brother Oscar and I walked to Salem Street. Car fare cost a dime, and there were not enough dimes to go around. Our new tenement was nice, but I missed the old neighborhood and playing jump rope and hopscotch with my friends. I missed Nick's Spa on the corner of Canterbury and Litchfield Streets where my sisters and I bought penny candy. My favorite was licorice and root beer barrels. Sometimes in winter we would get a cup of hot cocoa in heavy white mugs. I missed the bridge, the railroad tracks, the sight and sound of moving trains, and the lonely wail of the train whistle in the wee hours of the morning.

*L*iving close to the railroad tracks as a child may have influenced my writings in later years. My first piece of fiction, *Memories of a Christmas Past*, was published in the 1995 issue of *Miraculous Medal Magazine*. The story revolves around the railroad tracks, the forty-eight-step bridge; the hobos who rode the rails, and the breadlines during the Depression.

Our father was always looking for better tenements, so we moved around a lot. Our next house was on Austin Street. In those days I did not realize that there was life beyond Austin Street and downtown, let alone that there was a place such as Union Station in close proximity, until my sister Lillian and I took the train to visit the McKenzies in Brockton. I remember Union Station's vast interior with its shiny

Idamay Arsenault and three of her siblings. At bottom foreground, Roseanna, right, and Marcelle. In back, Idamay at left with Angelina.

black benches and the giant locomotive that spewed steam like a fierce dragon as it started its journey.

If memory serves, there was a step-stool to get onto the steps of the train, but I still needed help to board the train. Once we were seated, the conductor came around and punched our tickets. When the train picked up speed, I felt like I was going on an exciting adventure. We returned via Union Station and took the trolley home.

In those days, my life revolved around family, school, church, and the fun of playing kick-the-can, red rover, hide and seek, tag, ball and jacks, and marbles. On weekends, we would stage tap-dancing recitals on our side porch. Admission: One-Cent. Our teachers were our neighbors, Beverly Walker, Annette DeLaurier, and our sister Virginia, who took lessons from her friend, Doris Beauvais. We liked the idea of performing.

When we danced at our sister Lillian's wedding, the guests threw coins at our feet. When the crowd clapped for an encore, we were thrilled. We proceeded to do the same simple steps counting aloud, "One and two and three and four, five and six and seven and eight." Now, when we get together for Scrabble, my sisters and I reminisce and do the steps over again for laughs.

Another fun activity was roller-skating down the hill past Mrs. Hovey's house, around the corner onto Irving Street to Chandler Street. The four of us skating by her house at the same time equaled thirty-two noisy wheels. She yelled at us not to roller-skate by her house, but we did not heed her threats. One day she showered us with a pail of cold water as we passed by. However, it did not stop us. We went right back the next day.

The Royal Theater on Main Street near Austin was our favorite haunt on Saturdays. As soon as we had saved up ten cents (we were always saving up), we went to see The Green Hornet serials. It was not the cleanest place in town, and there were mice scampering around, but that didn't bother us.

The Worcester of those days was slow-moving and fun. My sisters and I sauntered around town on the way to Holy Family School on Orange Street, near where the main branch of the Worcester Public Library now stands. We especially liked window shopping on the way to school. We would walk down Austin Street, cut through the Post Office, go by

The Royal Theater in the rumble seat era.

the Palace Theater; cross Federal Street and proceed on Main Street until we got to the Mayflower Doughnut Shop across from Denholm & McKay's Department Store. As we peeked in the window, the smell of frying doughnuts wafted by us each time patrons opened the door. One day a decal in the window caught my eye:

> As you ramble on through life, brother,
> Whatever be your goal,
> Keep your eye upon the doughnut
> And not upon the hole.

To tell the truth I didn't know what it meant, I just liked the way it sounded. I have since come upon another little ditty much like it:

> Twixt the optimist and the pessimist
> The difference is droll
> The optimist sees the doughnut
> The pessimist sees the hole.

In the afternoon, upon returning from school, we would sometimes cut through the alley that led to the rear of Filene's Department Store and pick up empty boxes the store was throwing away. We used them to store trinkets and other assorted stuff. There was a pet shop on Myrtle Street across from the side of the Post Office. Sometimes we would stop there and knock on the windows to get the attention of a giant parrot and the cute little monkeys.

The shop owner was an old grouch and he would wave his arms, yelling for us to stop banging on his windows. We were foot-loose and fancy-free. We moseyed on home swinging our schoolbags, laughing and kicking stones to see who could kick them the farthest.

After my sister Roseanna and I made our Confirmation at Notre Dame Church, we had our pictures taken with our mother on the Common. We then crossed Main Street at Franklin, went by Denholm's and Richard Healey's; our white veils flying in the breeze, eager to get to Kresge's Five & Ten. A ten-cent

The author (left) with her mother and sister, Roseanna, after receiving Confirmation at Notre Dame des Canadiens.

strawberry ice cream cone was our present. We were happy as clams.

In the ensuing years, we moved many more times, but the most beautiful home we ever lived in was at 479 Park Avenue, a Queen Anne style house that we rented for several years during the forties. Sad to say, it met with the wrecking ball in 1998, to the dismay of our family and others who had lived in that area.

Now, as I pass the site, I see nothing but an unsightly mess — a dumpster and old cars parked among the weeds grown tall since the house was demolished — a blight to the neighborhood.

My three sisters and I graduated grammar school and high school. We were anxious to get out of school, find jobs, get married and have children. Not one of us even thought about going to college. Thus, we became the typical women of the 1950s. We got married, had children, stayed home, and were perfectly happy in our roles as housewives and mothers. We were what the Betty Friedan's would write about in their books about women's lib, to let us know what a terrible life we had. Well, we are none the worse for wear, and if we had to do it over again we would do it the same way.

The author, left, and her friend Jeanette Roy in the 1940s outside the Michaud home at 479 Park Avenue.

The author's brother, Eddy, in the parlor at 479 Park Avenue.

In 1942, my future husband Jerry,
boarded the train at Union Station as an
inductee into the U.S. Army
Infantry, and returned to the station for
a visit home before he went overseas.

Chapter Three

A majestic steam engine at Union Station in the 1930s. The tower of the old station is in the background.

Union Station in Peace and War

*U*nion Station was alive with servicemen either coming home on leave or leaving for their bases, not knowing if they would ever return. *The Worcester Evening Gazette* had a column announcing the names of those who were killed in action and another column for those missing in action. We hated to look for fear we would see the names of someone we knew.

It was a sad time; yet, people were filled with patriotic zeal.

It was a time of rationing. There were stamps for sugar, meat, and gasoline, and it was a time when servicemen and women were held in high regard. A time when you would give your seat to a serviceman or woman on the trolley or bus. They were our heroes. Once, while watching a movie at the Palace Theater, a loud voice from the stage announced that all army personnel in the audience must report for duty at once. The audience gave the exiting soldiers a round of applause.

Defense Plants were booming, and those who worked in them earned big money. I worked at Norton Company in the Diamond Wheel Division office. I did not want to get my hands dirty. Nevertheless, no matter how much or how little we earned, the boys paid twenty dollars a week for room and board, and the girls paid fifteen dollars. When I realized that office work didn't pay enough, I opted to work the night shift at St. Pierre Chain as a lady welder, welding anchor chains for the Navy. That job lasted six weeks. I had to ask the guy in the next aisle to crank the chains over to make room for the next set of chains. I left St. Pierre Chain and took a long leave of absence to recuperate.

The author in a high school photo.   Gerard Arsenault in a WW II photo.

In 1942, my future husband Jerry, boarded the train at Union Station as an inductee into the U.S. Army Infantry, and returned to the station for a visit home before he went overseas.

In January 1944, Jerry froze both feet in the watery trenches at Anzio, a small seaport on the western coast of Italy; the site of a major battle during World War II. An experimental sympathectomy operation (an alternative to amputation) was performed at the 21st Army General Hospital in Naples, by a German surgeon named Dr. Schumacher. Jerry returned home on the hospital ship, USS Seminole, and while crossing the Mediterranean Sea, he could see the smoke rising from the eruption of Mount Vesuvius.

A second operation was performed at Percy Jones General Hospital in Battle Creek, Michigan, by another German surgeon, Dr. Schwartz. Fortunately, both operations were successful.

When Jerry was discharged from the hospital nine months later, he arrived in Worcester via Union Station. He took a taxi home and surprised his parents, who had no idea he was coming home.

My second encounter at Union Station was in June of 1945, when my steady Jerry and I traveled from Worcester to visit his Aunt Alice in Mexico, Maine.

In those days, unmarried Catholic couples would never think of traveling overnight by themselves. Consequently, Jerry's mother came along to chaperone. It was a sweltering day, and it seemed to take an eternity to get to our destination. Jerry's uncle Damas picked us up in his rattletrap Hudson, and we arrived at their house exhausted. I dreaded the return trip, and swore I would never travel anywhere by train again — I never did. However, the trip was worth it. When Jerry's mother and aunt were busy in the kitchen, Jerry took advantage of our few minutes by ourselves. He proposed, and I said, "Yes."

*U*nion Station was still operational through the 1950s and 1960s, but during that period it closed in the evenings after the last train arrived. Passengers were accosted by thugs and teenage vandals, and it was no longer safe to use the station. When the station finally closed in 1972, it appeared that Worcester's sick-looking landmark was 'breathing its last.' It had

Worcester Telegram & Gazette photo

The honored dead of World War II return home via Union Station.

35

become a hangout for drug addicts, the homeless, and derelicts. It was also a great temptation for those who 'just wanted a souvenir'.

It was not until the spring of 1994, while taking a photography course at The Worcester Center for Crafts that I became interested in Union Station. After reading newspaper articles that predicted the station's certain demise, my interest peaked. I began shooting photos of the station for posterity.

When I read articles with negative comments about Union Station, I was annoyed. And remarks such as: "Why don't they just knock it down and make a parking lot for God's sake?" Or: "When is this city going to get rid of that eyesore?" made me angry.

Worcester Historical Museum photo

Doughboys outside Union Station during World War I.

wanted to take more photos of the station, but I feared going there alone, so I asked my nephew Eddy to accompany me as my bodyguard. There were strange characters roaming about, but I felt safe with a six-foot-two bouncer by my side. During our visit, we spotted a derelict picking up trash and putting it in a grocery cart filled with assorted stuff, all the while peering at us suspiciously from the corner of his eye.

Eddy was quite taken with the building, and he kept suggesting good spots to shoot. After he posed for a photo on the bench below the faded old barber shop sign, he talked me into exploring the right side of the building where a set of stairs led to an opening in a wall. We both peeked in and saw nothing but a big black hole. Suddenly, a big burly guy appeared from the shadows. When he saw my camera, he scurried back into the darkness like an animal running from a predator. "I'm out of here," I shouted, as I ran quickly down the flight of stairs. I had enough of Union Station for a while. But as we left, we both wondered aloud why such a beautiful building was left to rot, and I continued to take photos of the station for the next two years.

Eddy Picard sits in an alcove of Union Station in 1994.

Despite the put downs in the newspapers, to me Union Station was a wonderful place that had fallen on hard times. It had been a beautiful, majestic building, a true Worcester landmark. Now, it needed to be restored — not destroyed. It seemed impossible, but I hoped that someday something special would happen — that a knight in shining armor would come to the rescue of the grand old lady in distress. Almost no one thought it could happen — but it did.

Enter The Worcester Redevelopment Authority by way of The Worcester Center for Crafts.

We both peeked in and saw nothing but a big black hole. Suddenly, a big burly guy appeared from the shadows. When he saw my camera, he scurried back into the darkness like an animal running from a predator.

Chapter Four

The Good, the Bad, and the Scary

The author, with camera in hand, outside Union Station.

One of the good things about taking photography classes at The Worcester Center for Crafts with Peter Faulkner, is that I got some profitable leads there. One day as we were discussing a photo in the Telegram & Gazette taken by Betty Jenewin, Faulkner said that the photographer was a former student of his. Shortly after that conversation a photo of Union Station's interior by Jenewin appeared on the front page of the T&G. BOING!!! I called Jenewin and asked her how she was able to obtain access to the inside of the station. She gave me the name and number of Julie Sanders at the WRA, and I was in business.

Another time, Faulkner suggested that I enter the Intergenerational Photography Contest at Worcester State College. As he held up the flyer announcing the three monetary prizes, he said, "You could win some money." I noted that the deadline for submissions was the very next day. "Oh, I don't

By 1994, interior arches had fallen into disrepair.

know," I said, holding my chin and contemplating the matter.

Driving home from class, the wheels began to turn in my head. "Hmmm," I pondered. In-ter-gen-er-a-tion-al. Tricky theme. What did I have in my collection of negatives that I could develop, print, matte and frame by the next day?

As I looked through my proof sheets, one particular photo struck me like a bolt of lightning. Of course! A photo of Union Station's dilapidated roof in the foreground with the Worcester Common Fashion Outlets sign in the background. Perfect! The old and the new!

Union Station built in 1911, and the Fashion Outlets sign, 1995. I got excited. But first things first.

Five o'clock. Supper time. I opened a can of B&M beans.

I put the contents in a casserole; doctored them up with a glob of molasses and a teaspoon of brown sugar; cut up some franks, fried them, tossed them over the beans and, Voila! The dish was ready to pop in the microwave at a moment's notice. I set the table and ran to the darkroom.

In thirty minutes the print was drying. The matted and framed photo was ready just short of deadline the next day. Well, guess what? I came in a second-place tie and won two-hundred fifty dollars for my efforts. I was stunned, as well as grateful to Faulkner for the suggestion.

The bad part of taking photos of Union Station was that I had to travel to treacherous Washington Square and battle the Indy 500 hopefuls, each time hoping I'd survive one more trip. However, the most disconcerting part happened one miserable, slippery, snowy day, when I decided to park in the Municipal Parking lot across from the N.E.D. COR building. Without realizing it, I parked in a handicapped parking space. Then I huffed

Broken windows above the Post Office Door.

41

and I puffed my way to the station to shoot outdoor photos. Snow covered the sidewalks forcing me to walk in the street. When I returned to the parking lot I had a ticket on my windshield. Mad? You bet. I could not imagine why that happened. Me, one of the most conscientious citizens in Worcester - and I got a ticket!

The next day I returned to the exact spot, camera in hand, and took photos of the site, while in full view of three cruisers parked at the Kenmore Diner across the street. I was out to prove a point. I planned on appealing the ticket and prove my innocence. However, that night the darkroom told another story.

As I focused and enlarged the photo, I saw the evidence. Barely visible to the naked eye was part of the outline of a handicapped symbol on the pavement. I had not noticed it, or I would not have parked there. Grudgingly, I paid the fifty dollar fine. It would have been useless to plead for mercy.

After granting my request to shoot photos indoors, Julie

A deteriorating lion stares down from the front of Union Station.

Sanders of the WRA and I dodged the traffic to get to the station. A close-up of the station's facade exposed a disturbing sight. Stubborn green foliage had forced its way through open cracks everywhere. The lion head sculptures sprouted assorted greenery from their crevices; curly green growths clung to the arches of the bare windows boasting their own unique designs. One of the arched windows appeared to have a gray ghost-like figure against the coal black background of the stations' interior. Here and there cement steps had become dislodged from their moorings exposing stringy damp dirt dangling from the underpinnings. "Ugh!" I thought. I wondered what awaited us inside.

The station was deserted. I was stunned by what I saw. What was once a grand and beautiful interior was nothing but an eerie empty shell, totally stripped of its former elegance. Not at all like the station I remembered as a child. It had an open-air roof. Mounds of crumbled plaster and debris lay strewn upon the floor. Puddles of water were everywhere. The triple arches on each side of the waiting room stood

There we were on the edge of the roof of the Worcester Gear Works Building on Grafton Street with a bird's-eye view — taking shots of Union Station's dilapidated roof. After a snowstorm, I went up there again by myself. It was freezing cold, and the roof was glare ice. I teeter-tottered across to get a good shot of the snow-covered roof, and teeter-tottered right back. The result was this shot.

defiant as if to prove they still had staying power. When I asked Sanders how the building's main structure held up so well over the years, she said, "Because it was built like Fort Knox."

It was cold and damp. I began to have second thoughts about continuing my photography project. Maybe I should just shoot serene scenery or flower gardens, I thought, but my adventurous side won out and I pressed on. Nervously, I set up my tripod hoping that parts of the roof would not come cascading down and destroy my Nikkormat FT2 — never mind harming Sanders or me. I shot a roll of film as Sanders watched.

$\mathcal{T}$he scary part happened during my second visit to the station. Julie Sanders had left. I wasn't crazy about being in that dank, dark dungeon by myself. My wild imagination took hold. What if someone was hiding around a corner, or upstairs waiting to do me in. Might ghosts of days of yore resent the fact that I was there, invading their privacy. I was fidgety, so I left early, hoping that the next time someone would accompany me.

But the next time, I was alone again. I had just shot half a roll of film when I heard a shuffling noise coming from the dark passages behind me. (Probably a rat!) I shot through the door, with my half-closed tripod and dashed across Washington Square like a demented creature, to the safety of the Protector Group building's parking lot.

Another time my sister Angie accompanied me for protection. She was visibly ill at easy in the eerie environment. She stayed near the exit as she watched me shoot. Suddenly, my camera jammed. End of shoot. Future visits weren't so scary when engineers arrived to begin work on the roof. Thereafter, I wore a yellow hard hat for protection from falling debris. The hard hat also gave me a feeling of belonging to the crew.

The most daring photo shoot happened when my fellow photographer Pat Fisher and I went to the roof of the NED COR building that towers over the station's track side. The plant manager guided us and suggested where to take good shots. (Probably wondering if we had both taken leave of our senses). There we were on the edge of the roof with a bird's

44

eye view of Worcester's sky taking shots of Union Station's dilapidated roof.

After a snowstorm, I went up there again by myself, but the plant manager did not accompany me. It was freezing cold and the roof was glare ice. I teeter-tottered across to get a good shot of the snow-covered roof, took a few shots and teeter-tottered right back. That was the end of my daring photo shoots.

That particular photo of the snow-covered roof is my favorite of all the photos I have taken of Union Station. It shows how the building has defied all manner of neglect, survived all kinds of weather, and still boasts intricate patterns and minute details of its original design. Watson & Huckle, I commend you (wherever you are) for designing such a beautiful building, and kudos to those responsible for building a fortress, a lasting monument that still graces Worcester at Washington Square.

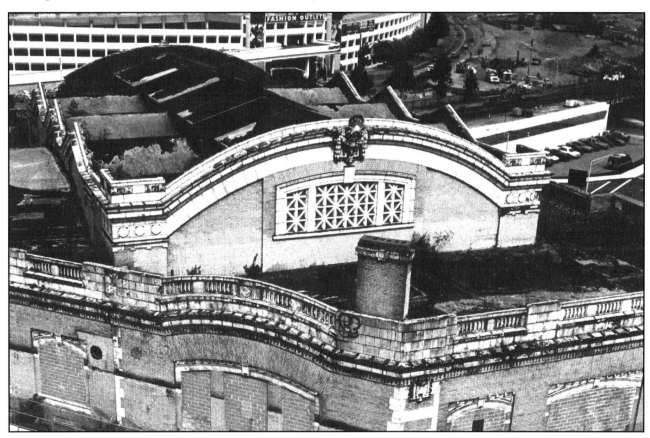

A prize-winning shot.

One day Rouleau decided to move on to greener pastures. He had been hearing about Worcester and its varied industries. He remembered the good impression the city had made on him, and at the end of June 1880, he returned to Worcester.

Chapter 5

The Gateway to a Dream

A French-Canadian Immigrant's Connection to Union Station — 1879

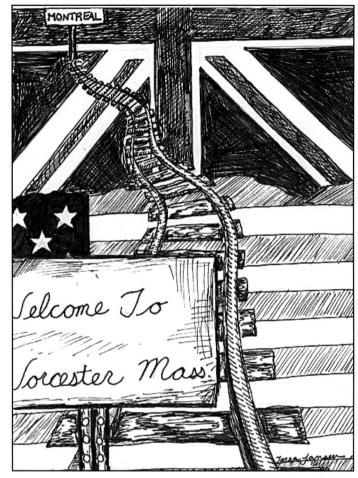

Sketch by Terra Jansen

n April of 1998, I was asked by Mr. Marcel Raymond, host of L'Heure Francaise radio program (WCUW) to do a presentation at Our Lady of Mound Carmel Recreational Center about French Canadians, with a link to Worcester's Union Station. Dr. Claire Quintal, Professor Emerita of French and Founder Directress Emerita of the French Institute at Assumption College in Worcester, suggested several books. I chose *Heritage of Peace, Land of Hope and Glory*, by Corinne Rocheleau Rouleau; later edited by her second cousin Louise Lind of Greenville, Rhode Island. It is based on the life of Wilfrid Rouleau, who is called Justin in the story.

The story unfolds in 1879, when a fourteen-year-old Canadian boy left his father's farm in St. Cuthbert, Canada, in search of a new life in the United States. With high hopes he bought a ticket to Chepachet, Rhode Island.

By the time Rouleau reached Montreal to board the train, he was already homesick. Not long after he had settled down in his seat, Rouleau was befriended by John B. Lucier, a railroad agent who lived in Worcester. Rouleau traveled alone from Montreal to Union Station in Worcester, Massachusetts. Those decades marked the greatest influx of French-Canadians to the United States. Montreal and Worcester became the two main stations in that exodus. Worcester's Union Station was known for years as *Le Depot de Monsieur Lucier*, because so many of the French-Canadians who entered the United States via this terminal benefited from the kindness of Mr. Lucier. When Rouleau got off the train in Worcester, he was just another member of a crowd milling around in the waiting room, a bunch of bedraggled, weary and hungry strangers, a sorry sight in everyone's eyes.

Rouleau had a few hours to kill before the train to Providence was due and he decided to look around Worcester. He was very impressed by the city. But when he reached Chepachet, Rouleau was not the least bit impressed by the tiny hamlet that consisted only of two mills, a general store, and some rundown houses where the mill workers lived. And that was all there was of Chepachet. Rouleau stayed with a family that came from the same part of Quebec as he did.

As Rouleau walked the streets that first day, loud whistles started to blast from the mills. He couldn't believe his eyes as he watched women coming out of the mills looking down-hearted and weary, their children walking behind them exhausted from their day's work, with tufts of cotton wool sticking to their clothes, their hair, and their faces. Women and children were hired as cheap labor. That was a common occurrence in those days, and they worked from sunup to sundown six days a week, while the husbands stayed home, smoked their pipes and did the housework. Soon disenchanted, Rouleau decided to leave for Woonsocket, a city about nine miles away. He left Chepachet, never to return.

Unlike Chepachet, Woonsocket was a bustling city with houses and mills clustered along the Blackstone River. It was a welcome sight to Rouleau. There he lived with the Fauteux family, former neighbors from St. Cuthbert. While teaching in Monsieur Drainville's school for a year, he lived with the schoolmaster. He was pleased that the city government frowned upon child labor.

One day Rouleau decided to move on to greener pastures. He had been hearing about Worcester and its varied industries. He remembered the good impression the city had made on him, and at the end of June 1880, he returned to Worcester.

On detraining a second time in Worcester, the first thing Rouleau noticed was a crowd of newly arrived Canadians. They were a sorry sight, bedraggled and weary. It was a deja vu of his arrival in Worcester less than a year before.

At first he found work in a shop making screws. Later he became a gun polisher, then he worked for Le Courier, a French daily newspaper. Finally, after an apprenticeship in a print shop Rouleau decided that journalism would be his life's work.

He found a temporary job with the Worcester Evening

Gazette at $8 a week. He also helped to set type for the very first copy of the Worcester Telegram. Rouleau bought his first suit at the Ware Pratt Store. He felt proud as he walked into Notre Dame Church and joined the ranks of the well-dressed gentlemen at Sunday Mass. Rouleau loved the Worcester of that period, a city large enough to have many facets, but not too large to retain a fine simplicity and ease of life. But, Rouleau was ambitious and there were still more worlds to conquer. At age twenty-one, he left Worcester to begin a new phase of his life in New York City where he was to learn more about the printing trade. He returned a year later to marry the girl of his dreams and they went back to New York. In 1890, Rouleau went to work in Lowell, Massachusetts, for Josiah Quincy and the newspaper syndicate supporting the Democratic Party. In 1893, he worked in Washington, D.C. for the US Government Printing Office.

Both Wilfrid Rouleau and Corinne Rocheleau were in their middle years when, after the first Mrs. Rouleau's death, they were married. They lived in the then small and delightful suburb of Washington called Brookland. This was close to Wilfrid's work and to his only child, Louis.

After Rouleau's retirement from the United States Government Printing Office, he and his wife Corinne, went to Montreal to live in retirement quarters at Corinne's alma mater,

Wilfrid Rouleau in 1881.

a school for deaf-mutes. (Corinne had become a deaf-mute as a young child).

Louis Rocheleau, an aviator in World War I, became a prominent Washington architect and the father of four sons. Corinne's father was a well-to-do businessman of wide acquaintance and diverse business activities throughout New England. Both of her parents were leaders in the large and growing community of French Canadians in Worcester who had come down from eastern Canada during the last half of the nineteenth century. In the prologue of *Heritage of Peace, Land of Hope and Glory*, Charles A. Rocheleau, nephew of Corinne Rocheleau writes:

It may come as a complete surprise to many readers that millions of North Americans are of French origin and that, even today, many still speak French. People of French ancestry are particularly numerous throughout New England. They are usually indistinguishable from their fellow citizens of other ancestries. They speak the same English as their neighbors but often in New England, lapse into French with family or other known bilingual persons. As can be seen a bit through the saga of Wilfrid Rouleau, these citizens have definite French traits that enrich and refine the American character: Acceptance of other people's ideas, individualism in

Commander Charles A. Rocheleau, USN (Retired) with his niece and her husband — "Chuck and Mud."

Charles A. Rocheleau

Rippon, West Virginia

The first time I saw the old Worcester Railroad Station, which was built in 1875, was in the early 1900s. (I was born in 1913.) Only a small portion of it was left. But the tall high and blackened stone (I believe granite) tower impressed my young eyes indeed. As I recall a remnant of the station itself was still extant and used for freight purposes. The new and present station had replaced it as a passenger terminal. The bright new station with its white marble and two smaller towers of very different architecture was in stark contrast to the smoky tower of the old station.

My grandfather, Henri Louis Rocheleau and my own father, Henri Oscar, both used the old and then the new station for almost daily trips to and from Boston where my grandfather was a partner in the firm of Rhodes and Ripley, manufacturers of men's clothing with the main office in Boston. My grandfather and my father, a young salesman for the firm traveled all over the United States. But Henri Louis died in 1900 and my father, a very young married man with two children had to take over the business of

everything, including politics, a penchant for intellectual pursuits such as the arts and all aspects of...the joie de vivre.

Commander Charles A. Rocheleau, USN (Retired) now in his mid-eighties, is alive and well at this writing. His memories of Union Station follow.

his father in Boston and management of three retail men's clothing stores which he had also organized. It must be remembered that the railroad station was the key to transportation to Boston and other large U.S. cities. There was really no wide use of the automobile until after World War I and no modern, well-maintained highways. In fact many roads were not even paved. There were no buses and no passenger planes such as we have today. There were horse-drawn wagons and electric-powered street cars. Each morning at 8 a.m. a large group of men, who lived in Worcester, including my father (there were few women) would converge on the station for the hour's ride.

The same group arrived back at 6 p.m. During the ride back many of them paired off to play cards. The regulars and the train personnel knew each other and enjoyed the conviviality. My father loved to play cards on the train.

Each of the boys in our family embarked at the station for a rail trip to Boston at a very early age. When we arrived at the Columbus Avenue and Washington Street Rhodes and Ripley office, my father would let us loose for the day and he told us to return at 4:30 p.m. for the ride back to Worcester. We had full freedom to explore

the city with its golden-domed capitol. I learned to orient myself in its crooked maze of streets, and to buy things to eat and get back to the office at 4:30 for the grand ride back home.

Coming out of the terminal, the scene was totally different from today. Across the way were one or two hotels, a saloon, and conveyances coming up for the returning passengers. One could walk up Front Street to Main Street (unimpeded by the present day shopping mall) and pass all kinds of stores; the Insane Asylum (where the Federal Post Office is now) and then the Worcester County Jail and the large Victorian Sheriff's residence (where I once lived after the great Depression). Now all is gone. WHAT A TIME. WHAT A DIFFERENCE.

Note: Rocheleau's sister-in-law, Anne Rocheleau, is Worcester's well-known concert pianist. Anne's daughter, known in show business as Mud is part of the popular Worcester singing duo, Chuck & Mud.

Heritage of Peace, Land of Hope and Glory, *may be purchased from Jemtech Digital Services, Publishers, 9 Elmwood Drive, Cumberland, RI 02864 Tel (401).333-0345.*

What began as a photography project soon turned into something more. The following two chapters present the memories of some of the people for whom Union Station played a special role. These stories really represent the Memories of the Monument.

Chapter Six

Sentimental Journeys

Harvey Ball

Worcester, Massachusetts

Many years before he created the Smiley Button, Ball recalls that Union Station was a very busy place. The station was a familiar spot for him in his earlier years. It was convenient to travel by rail and not expensive. He said he probably used it more during the World War II years when coming home on furlough from the army. He remarks that the Union Station of those days was neat, clean, and vibrant. Uniformed young men were always present with a small group of relatives to see them off or meet them as they arrived. Ball recalls a particular day when he took a local north to Ayer. He was reporting for active duty in the Army Air Corps as an aviation cadet. Six weeks earlier, he had been sworn in, and then told to go home and wait to be called. But they said that if he wanted to go earlier, to write a letter requesting an immediate call up. He did this after three weeks. But another three weeks passed before he received a letter to report.

ℒn order to get to Fort Devens by 7:30 in the morning, he had to take the local train at Union Station at 6 a.m. He caught a trolley at Park Avenue and Chandler Street at 5:30 a.m. and got to Union Station in time for his train. As early as it was, the station was very busy with lots of civilians and military personnel and a constant movement of people. He paid sixty cents for a ticket, headed north on the local, and went off to serve.

Actually, Ball does not think that many young men entering the service had to pay for their transportation to join.

Ball rose to the rank of colonel while serving in the Pacific under General MacArthur. Ball, the creator of the Smiley Face button, designed the world famous face as part of an advertising campaign for The State Mutual Life Assurance Company of America in Worcester (now Allmerica Financial). He was paid two hundred and forty dollars for his efforts, and that was the end of his monetary profit. Smart entrepreneurs in Japan made a bundle on the button according to a newspaper article, and many have gotten on the bandwagon since. But it is our own Worcester artist who painted the two oval black eyes and a whimsical smile on a banana-yellow background, that makes one smile at the sight of the famous face.

Ball has been getting much publicity in the past few months to promote his button, and most recently a Worcester Historical Museum newsletter boasts a Smiley Christmas ornament in a limited edition.

On October 1, 1999, Worcester Common Fashion Outlets hosted World Smile Day to a large audience that included Mayor Raymond Mariano, City Manager Thomas Hoover, State Representative Harriet Chandler, and United States Congressman James McGovern's father, Walter F. McGovern, who spoke for his son who was in Washington.

Many other civic dignitaries occupied the chairs close to the stage. Students from Flagg Street School and the Seven Hills Charter School did an impressive presentation and sang songs written by Harvey's son Charles Ball in honor of Smiley.

The highlight of the event was the unveiling of the United States Postal Service commemorative America Smiles stamp, boasting the Smiley Face.

Carol (Moran) Bibaud

Worcester, Massachusetts

Carol Bibaud with her husband, Charles.

My mother, sister and I went to Union Station to board a train for Mississippi. My Dad was in the Army and we were on our way to visit him. This was during World War II. I was only six-years-old and in awe over the large, high ceiling building. I was so impressed that it had a barbershop with a candy-striped pole. It was my first train ride. The station was very crowded because of it being war time. I recall sitting on someone's lap the entire trip.

Many years later as a young bride, Bibaud was back at Union Station boarding a train to meet her husband who was in the Army, stationed in Maryland. They would meet in New York City for a few days together. The last time Bibaud visited Union Station was to welcome her husband home for good — that was forty-two years ago.

Martin M. Cariglia

Worcester, Massachusetts

On October 2, 1954, Corp. Martin M. Cariglia of 254 Shrewsbury Street is greeted at Union Station by his wife Lucy, and eight-month old son, Martin Joseph, whom he saw for the first time. Mrs. Cariglia is the sister-in-law of John Evangelista, owner of the Parkway Diner.

Antonette Clemons

Shrewsbury, Massachusetts

During the thirties Antonette Clemons lived in Winchendon, and the only way she could visit her folks was by train by way of Union Station, then taking a cab up to Ingleside Avenue.

The whole trip did not cost two dollars as she remembers. When her husband left for boot camp training during World War II, she borrowed her neighbor's Ford and took him to Union Station to get a train bound for Finger Lakes, New York. She recalls that it was a very busy place at that time.

Clemons is an avid reader of novels, and enjoys writing letters to her grandchildren and to her daughter, Wendy, who lives in Alaska.

Marcelle (Dumas) Carter

Shrewsbury, Massachusetts

My fond memories of Union Station date back to 1943 when I was nine years old. Many a Sunday afternoon my father packed us in the family car, my mother, my two sisters Jeanne and Cecile, and drove to Union Station. The reason being, they wanted to sit in the station and watch the servicemen coming home on furlough from the war. Hoping upon hope that one of my two brothers might be one of the servicemen getting off the train.

My two brothers were in the Marines, one stationed in the South Pacific, fighting on the front lines, and one was stationed in the States. Neither had been home since they left to do their tour of duty. My mother wrote to them every single day.

I remember my sister and I playing in and out and around the long wooden benches in what I thought was a huge station. I also remember the station being crowded with soldiers coming and going, with families saying good-bye and some happy to see them coming home.

My mother was always sad on the drive home because my brothers were never one of the Marines getting off the train. But, each Sunday we would return to Union Station in great anticipation.

In 1953, my classmates and I from Shrewsbury High left from Union Station to go on our class trip to New York and Washington. At that time the building was still big and impressive. I remember the platform and the carts that carried the luggage.

Ed Cournoyer,

Grafton, Massachusetts

Ed Cournoyer skipped school many times to go to Union Station. He recalls that Union Station was a great place to hang around with his friends to meet some girls. However, when the establishment got sick of them hanging around they kicked them out.

At age fourteen, Cournoyer was forced to quit school to go to work. He worked with his father driving team to support the family of ten children. He remembers the roundhouse located in back of Union Station used to turn the engines around at the end of a run. He also recalls hanging around Harrington Corner during the winter, and when it got too cold, he and his friends would trek to Union Station to warm up. His other recollections are the Washington Hotel across from the station and the Front Street Market.

At age 17, during World War I Cournoyer left from Union Station with three of his buddies to join the Navy. He lied about his age, and didn't tell his parents anything about his plans. When the authorities discovered the lie they admonished him severely and made plans for him to return home, but not before he paid the price for his misdeeds by doing KP (kitchen police) duty.

During World War II at age forty-four, Cournoyer was drafted. At the time he worked for the City Truck Company and just happened to be one of six best men the company employed and the company asked for a deferment which was granted.

At age ninety-six, Cournoyer lives alone and is sharp as a tack. He attributes his longevity to eating well, loving people, and having a good nature.

James Cournoyer

Worcester, Massachusetts

James Cournoyer holding the brick and horse tie he found at Union Station

*J*ames Cournoyer, nephew of Ed Cournoyer, (above) a master plumber who worked at Union Station's restoration work writes:

I left the station last June and had been working on the Med City job. I visited the station back in November. The ceiling panels had been hung. It was breathtaking to see. Not only was it beautiful but it has become an architectural feat in itself. My hat goes off to everybody involved in the remake of Union Station. Just think, it's not too often that a building like this is brought back to life again. The people of Worcester will soon realize all of this.

The brick that I found inscribed "ANNESS & MULLER, BOSTON No.1 LCI," is yellow in color. It appears to be a fire brick. According to the city of Worcester map dated 1896 there were buildings on the lot before the station was built. The brick was probably from a fireplace. It was dug up about four feet in the basement floor. It appeared to be from a fireplace that was somewhat still intact. We also found a large grinding wheel, some old china cups and plates that were in good condition. We were below the Grand Hall when we found these items. We also dug up some old bottles. I kept one bottle that is from the Hotel Rialto. It has a name on it called Matt Kennedy. According to the map the hotel was located on 257 Front Street. I heard the Rialto

Hotel was torn down to make room for the station. I also found a horse tie in the back of the building. One thing is for sure — this building has a lot of character and charm.

One last note about Union Station. I have been a Plumber for twenty-three-years. I've worked on many buildings. This building is a Fortress!! The footing is solid granite that is fifty-four inches thick. The inside walls are made of brick and average thirty-one inches thick. This is one solid building. I found the following information at the Worcester Historical Museum.

Matthew J. Kennedy, Hotel proprietor and wholesale merchant was born in West Boylston, Massachusetts, July 8, 1855, son of Patrick and Ellen (Yates) Kennedy. He became proprietor of the Rialto Hotel, which became popular among traveling salesmen visiting Worcester. He continued in business for fourteen years. At the time of the changed grades of the railroads, the property was purchased for railroad purposes.

Linda Darling

Worcester, Massachusetts

I have always loved photography and seemed to have an eye for some things. I had taken several classes at the Worcester Art Museum when I was a teenager and really grew a passion for it. In 1977, while a sophomore at South High School, photography was the only class I enjoyed and got a passing grade in. I used to skip my other classes and pretended I had permission to work in the darkroom.

One assignment we had was an "architectural" photo essay. I tried shooting several buildings like Clark University and some tall buildings in the downtown area, but I wasn't very satisfied. It wasn't planned to go to Union Station, I just sort of happened upon it, noticed it, and became very intrigued by the outside, and I just had to go in to see what else might be there. It was pretty scary, but very exciting and thrilling to be in this place where "danger and warning" signs were displayed.

I was a very bold teenager, so needless to say, that did not stop me. It intrigued me all the more. It was so desolate, dark, and very dusty with only scarce rays of sunshine poking

Linda Darling photo

The state of disrepair in 1977.

through. I convinced my friend to venture in with me and we explored quite a few areas. We must have scared "them" while I was taking pictures, because we saw two men run out of the building.

We were scared also so we went out to the tracks to take some more shots. My teacher was upset that I went into such a dangerous area, but he was very impressed with the shots. He loved the graininess, contrast, and composition which earned me an "A."

60

Mario DeMarco

West Boylston, Massachusetts

As a young newspaper boy Mario DeMarco had many memorable experiences at Union Station. When Tom Mix, the famous rodeo and cowboy star made a personal appearance there with his horse Tony, DeMarco stood in awe that he was actually seeing the movie star in the flesh. "Oh, Tom Mix," he sighed, as his mouth fell open; gaping, hardly believing his eyes.

As Tom Mix looked down at the crowd from a high platform to a square full of people (about 5,000) they urged him to jump down, and just as he was about to do it his agent stopped him for fear they would mob him. Mix usually wore a white western outfit — with a specially made white Stetson. His horse Tony had a white patch on his face; a beautiful horse with four white-stocking legs. Gene Autry used a horse (Champion) similar to Tony.

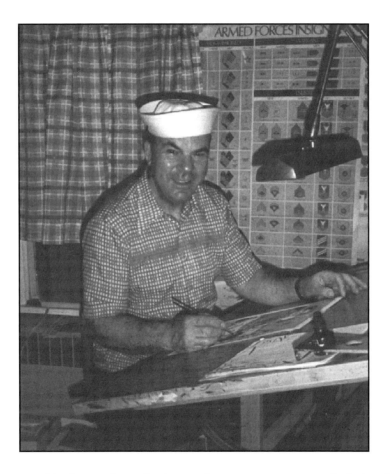

Another time Ken Maynard, a major western star, appeared at Union Station. DeMarco reminisces about when Maynard ate at Union Lunch directly across from the station on Harding Street.

After World War II when Ike Eisenhower campaigned for the presidency, DeMarco saw and met Ike underneath in back of the station, where US mail and other parcels were delivered and shipped out. As a boy I used to pick up the Boston Record newspapers there. That area was used mostly for parking. Time was when you got a lot for your money. During the Depression newspapers sold for two-cents. A shoe shine stand in the main lobby charged a nickel for a shine. A haircut cost somewhere around a dollar-fifty. DeMarco remembers talking to the porters, who he said were very friendly and helpful in many ways.

DeMarco and his brother would race to the telephone booths every morning to see if there were some nickels in the wells. Many times after selling papers during the days and nights they used the big friendly station to warm up between selling papers.

There were a maze of underground tunnels used to transport baggage but mostly for getting from one place to another. Union Station was used as a short-cut from Shrewsbury Street to Green Street. From Green Street where the PNA club is now there is a sealed-up entrance that led to Shrewsbury Street.

DeMarco also remembers the snow trains. They were used to plow snow from the tracks. Pity the cows who got in the way of an oncoming snow train. These trains were nick-named cow catchers.

"I loved sports and westerns — we even produced pictures when youngsters," relates DeMarco, who eventually became a cartoonist/writer for sports and western magazines.

At present, DeMarco is freelancing at his leisure. Some of his books are on Charles Starrett, Tom Mix, Gene Autry, Roy Rogers, John Wayne, Gabby Hayes, and many others.

DeMarco worked for the Navy Times in Washington, D.C. as a cartoonist, has written a book about ships and another on Naval Air Squadrons. He's had a busy life and hopes to continue on as such.

"Idamay has chosen a good subject — Union Station," DeMarco says, "and I'm quite sure there are hundreds of people who have fond and pleasant memories of this great place. I wish her loads of good luck. I don't know if the new station could ever equal the colorful old one, but let's give it a try."

The Donnelly's

The Donnelly brothers, from left, Bill, Ray Jr. and Jack. At right, a photo of their father, Raymond E. Donnelly Sr., one of the last of Union Station's station masters.

William C. Donnelly

Hudson, Florida

*W*illiam Donnelly is one of three sons of Raymond E. Donnelly, one of Union Station's last Stationmasters who worked there for forty-seven years. The elder Donnelly walked to work every day from his home on Barkley Street. Raymond's brother Walter, and Walter's son Ralph, both were conductors on the Boston to Worcester run for many years and both also retired from the railroad.

As a teenager, William once worked at Union Station during the Christmas rush. His older brother Ray Jr., worked there for one year.

Alma (Vigneault) Dumaine

Auburn, Massachusetts

ℐn winter there was always snow up to the windowsills." Says Alma Dumaine. She lived on Ball street in Worcester all her life with her parents, her sister, and three brothers.

Dumaine's fondest teenage memories are those good old days at the Union Station. On many a cold and snowy Sunday morning Dumaine and her friends Rose, Aurora, Louise and Betty Frappier, took a ride on the snow train at Union Station for a day on the slopes of Mount Snow in Vermont.

"We were not the best skiers but we sure made an effort to stay up. There were a lot of young boys and girls there, but I always liked to mingle with the boys. We enjoyed the trips and everyone was out for a real friendly good time." says Dumaine.

An outgoing woman in her teens, and still is at eighty-three, she got a job advertising Target cigarette tobacco in store windows, but not until she begged the company boss to hire her. He gave her the excuse that she was too young and that she'd have to be on the road, but Dumaine persisted with a sob story. "I really need this job, because m-my father is out of work, and..." Dumaine got the job. At first she sat in the window at Buffington's Drug Store on Main Street, and then she traveled with the boss to Woonsocket, Rhode Island, Connecticut, Leominster, Marlboro, Hudson, and Ware, Mass., and earned $33.00 a week for the five-week tour.

A collector of Worcester memorabilia, Dumaine has postcards of Union Station among them. She also has movie star scrapbooks and song sheets from the 1940s and 1950s. An Elvis Presley fan for many years she has some interesting items, one of which is a magnet figure of Elvis on the fridge door.

Dumaine is grateful that Union Station is once again a glorious Worcester landmark.

Long before the Surgeon General became concerned about nicotine, Alma Vigneault advertised Target Cigarettes at Buffington's Drug Store on Main Street, Worcester.

Delena E. (Streeter) Fahey,

Worcester, Massachusetts

I fondly remember our family taking a yearly trip to Nantasket Beach which began at Union Station in Worcester. I was a young girl — probably about eight or nine years old, and every year I waited for and looked forward to taking this trip, and I was never disappointed. My mom packed a lunch of sandwiches, fruit, and snacks and we headed to Union Station.

As I recall, we walked through doors that were on street level or maybe one or two steps up. It was an awesome feeling to enter this gigantic area. It had a very high ceiling and there were several large

Delena (Streeter) Fahey as a youngster on a ferry going to Nantasket and in a recent photograph.

wooden pews that popped out at you as you entered. These pews are my most vivid memory of this majestic building. As I stated, the pews were wooden and they were highly polished and very conducive to sliding back and forth on if they weren't occupied by other people.

My dad would go to a ticket window to purchase our tickets from an employee who wore a large conductor-like hat. The only other thing that I recall about this large open area was a barber

shop located in a back corner. It had a red and white barber pole in front of it, and maybe that's why I remembered this.

When the train to Boston was announced, we would proceed to the back of the building and exit onto a platform from which we would board the train. We soon heard the booming voice of the conductor cry out, "All Aboard" and we were off.

We sat in two seats that faced each other, allowing our family to be together. The conductor, who always had a smile and a few words for each of us children, would soon be by to collect our fares.

It was an exciting ride which today unfortunately, is not experienced by many children.

We were on our way. We went through wooded areas and passed houses, towns, and people who waved to us as we went by. My parents would give us some snacks, but we were rarely hungry because there was so much to see both inside and outside of the train.

I think that it took a little over an hour to arrive in Boston. We then had to walk a short distance to Rowe's Wharf where we got onto a boat that took us to Nantasket Beach. We had our day at the beach, made our return trip on the boat and then took the train back to Union Station in Worcester. More than once we would doze off on the train being lulled by the clickety-clack of the wheels on the railroad track.

"I frequently ride by Union Station and it looks great. I hope to travel from there in the future." Fahey said.

An RSVP volunteer, Fahey puts in time at Worcester's Ecotarium doing various jobs such as organizing old slides of Worcester, stuffing envelopes, and working in any other area where she is needed.

Dan and Jessie Lie Farber

Worcester, Massachusetts

*D*an Farber of Worcester (deceased) remembers the days when it was possible to go into a store on Front Street and borrow a commuter's ticket book to Boston for a fee less than legal fare. Farber claims there were more than one of these illegal operators in the Front Street area.

When Farber was ten or twelve years old, he remembers traveling from Union Station to Boston with his father who was in the leather business. Once or twice he went with him to South Street. "There was one corner on South Street if you wanted to meet anyone in the leather business," Farber relates, "you'd be sure to see them because everyone in the leather business was in Boston."

As a young man Farber liked to watch trains. "One time I was on the tracks at Union Station watching the trains come and go. One train, traveling in reverse, approached me from my back. Fortunately, there was an attendant on the rear of the approach-

ing car. He rushed into the car and pulled the emergency switch. The train started to stop but was still approaching me. As it came closer the attendant hollered and I jumped to safety." said Farber.

"In the early days when Union Station was still a very busy place," Farber recalls, "planes had made their first inroads on the train traffic." One day while talking to one of the train ticket officers he was embarrassed to hear himself refer to his plane ticket rather than his train ticket.

Mr. Farber was an executive for many years in the business founded by his father, L. Farber Company, on Fremont Street. When the business sold in 1981, it was the largest supplier of shoe insoles and leather shoe welting in the United States.

Regrettably, Mr. Farber died in June of 1998. I consider myself most fortunate to have met this kind and gentle man, and deeply honored that he saw my photo exhibit, *State of the Union*, at the Rose Madder Gallery on Grove Street. I cherish the letter he wrote me that began: Congratulations on that fine show of Union Station pictures. Farber ended the letter with: I should be glad to hear from you. I enjoyed seeing your show.

Such accolades from a nationally acclaimed photographer who had 40,000 photographs in museums, including a collection of 15,000 in the American Antiquarian Society, twenty in the Worcester Art Museum, and the Library of Congress, is enough to keep this photographer on cloud nine 'til the end of time.

Generous beyond belief, I have in my possession twenty of Farber's color prints he gave me after the interview for this book. I have a photograph of Dan and his wife, Jessie Lie on my desk. When I get discouraged either with my photography projects or with my creative writing work, I stop and look at Dan's smiling face and I recall his uplifting words: Congratulations on that fine show of Union Station pictures.

Naomi Miller

Worcester, Massachusetts

N aomi Miller, Secretary to Dan and Jessie Farber, recalls that in 1944 she was in Worcester's Union Station. She thought it was beautiful. She came to Worcester because her husband-to-be who was in the service, traveled from Worcester to Providence. She remembers the station as being very busy and very, very attractive.

On a trip to Washington, D.C., she visited their Union Station and it was absolutely beautiful. Absolutely gorgeous. It is much bigger than Worcester's Union Station, but in some ways it's similar. However, it doesn't have the twin towers that makes our Union Station unique. It has a great big dome and it's tall. In fact Miller bought a postcard of Washington's Union Station, and hoped that Worcester's Union Station could be as beautiful.

Nicholas Gage

North Grafton, Massachusetts

Nicholas Gage, noted author of the novel Eleni, that later became a movie, recalls: "When I first arrived in America in 1949, my father worked at a restaurant across the street from Union Station called Terminal Lunch. Whenever I visited him I would walk across the street to the station and wander around its huge space. To me, it looked like one of the Greek Temples I saw in Athens, but fully restored. It had both majesty and simplicity that made it exciting to look at and be in."

"I traveled from the station a couple of times as a teenager. But by that time it was starting to lose its luster, and each time I went back it was sad to see how rapidly it was deteriorating."

"My most memorable experience occurred when I was eleven or twelve when I saw a woman in a yellow dress walking through the station who looked like a clone of Virginia Mayo, the object of my desire in my boyhood as Ava Gardner was in my youth. The image of the young woman, walking elegantly across the terminal like a dancer across a huge stage, has never faded from my memory."

Gage, a former investigative reporter and foreign correspondent for the New York Times, was born in Greece in 1939 and emigrated to the United States ten years later. In addition to Eleni, he is the author of five other books, two about Greece and three about organized crime.

Robert Goulet

Shrewsbury, Massachusetts

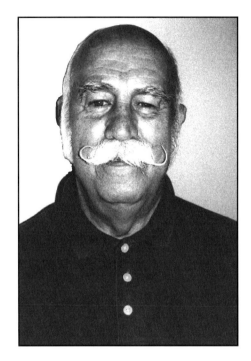

The only thing Robert Goulet of Shrewsbury has in common with the star of the 1960's musical, Camelot, is his clear blue eyes.

When Goulet was about eight years old he recalls going to Union Station and seeing Franklin Delano Roosevelt campaigning by train. Goulet had gone to Trumbull Square with his mother to shop at the market. After going by T.O. Flynn's horse stable they went into Union Station and up the stairs to the track side, and there was Roosevelt at the caboose end of the train talking to a large crowd of people. Goulet never forgot that experience.

The Railway Express parcel post building on the Franklin Street side of the station was a very busy place in those days. As a soldier during World War II, Goulet took the train from Union Station to go to Fort Devens.

"It was a nice station," Goulet recalls, "but it got to be an eyesore over the years. Now, as I look at the towers going up I'm really happy that Union Station is being restored."

Eva (Celularo) Kiley

Worcester, Massachusetts

Usually after attending one of the downtown movie houses, we would always stop in the Union Station to either use the bathrooms, buy a candy bar from the vendor, or sit on the long benches and pretended we were going on a trip - a pleasant experience. We also used to go up to the track section (which was against all railroad rules) and use it as a short-cut to get to Franklin Street.

We usually went to the Palace Theater which at that time cost ten cents, but the price later went up to twenty-five cents.

They sold refreshments, however, we were too poor to afford them. We usually brought our own snacks from home. My parents had ten children, so we considered ourselves lucky just to get the price of admission. We saw Tarzan movies, Esther William's swim movies, or at that time, many war movies. I can vividly recall seeing John Wayne in a film called, "Back to Batan."

During World War II the scene inside of the station was very sad as we watched our brothers go off to war.

I hope that the renovations are completed in my lifetime.

Gertrude Burns Lacey

Worcester, Massachusetts

s I entered Gertrude Lacey's living room I immediately felt at ease. A gracious white-haired lady with dancing blue eyes, she felt right at home talking about Union Station, no doubt because her family had always been railroad people.

Lacey was born in Princeton, Massachusetts in 1907. Her father, William Burns worked at the Princeton Depot as station agent in 1903 until his retirement in 1926. Her sister Mildred worked at the Lincoln Square freight office for many years as a telegraph officer, and Lacey was employed at Union Station under Mary Megan, secretary to James Sweeney, in the District Passenger Office from 1931 to 1934, where she earned $19.20 a week.

In those days Union Station was a very busy place. You could buy monthly tickets; a piece of cardboard punched by the conductor each time you boarded the train, but Lacey never had to pay for tickets, she got them free because she worked there.

Lacey remembers the inside of the station as being cool - a nice place to be

in the heat of summer. The porters kept the station shiny clean day in and day out. There was a large restaurant with white tablecloths, but Lacey didn't eat there because it was too expensive. She didn't eat at the counter either; she brought her own lunch. She recalls that a cup of coffee cost a nickel but it cost more if you had cream and sugar. That's how she got used to drinking her coffee black as she still does today.

The trains had sleeper bunks with paisley print cotton curtains that pulled across for privacy.

Lacey remembers seeing Al Smith, former governor of New York and Democratic nominee for President, wave to her as he passed by her office. Many times after work she would shop for her mother at the Front Street Market. A few doors down was Kennedy's where they sold butter and eggs.

Lacey has a collection of old photos of Worcester scenes, but her favorite is the one of her father at the Princeton Depot. She has a photo of the Eliot Swan's Hotel that was formerly on the site of the 1875 station across from where the present station now stands.

At ninety-two, Lacey admits she's not as active as she used to be. However, she still drives a car and takes time to go bowling at the Mill Street Bowling Alley once a week.

A long time RSVP volunteer, Lacey

Gertrude Lacey's father, William Burns, at the railroad station in Princeton, Massachusetts.

Photo courtesy of Gertrude Lacey

has been active with the Easter Seal Association for twenty-seven years, and continues to do volunteer work at Mechanics Hall. An avid golfer for many years, Lacey enjoyed attending the Pleasant Valley Golf Tournaments in Sutton. Skilled at crocheting, she has made such items as tablecloths, bedspreads, and dresses. She has three life-size stuffed dolls sitting pretty on couches in her living room. Her niece, Michelle creates them to cover upright vacuum cleaners, but Lacey likes them better on chairs. As a pastime Lacey reads novels and socializes with her nieces and nephews.

"Union Station," Lacey sighs, "it was such a beautiful place."

Edmond Laurence

Worcester, Massachusetts

"One thing I remember about trains in Worcester is that we lived about three or four hundred yards from the Boston & Albany railroad tracks on Lyman Street" said Laurence. On cold winter nights he could hear those train whistles announcing their arrival at the station. It seemed as though every five minutes there was a train, whether a freight train was coming by or a passenger train. There was the Boston & Albany, Providence & Worcester, the Boston & Maine, and they all merged in Worcester, Laurence recalls.

When he was a kid Laurence and his friends would sit on a big banking

overlooking the railroad tracks and when the trains came by they would wave at the conductor. A story went around that if any stones rolled down on the tracks when the train came by the conductor would stop the train dead on, get out and make them pick up all the stones and throw them back where they came from.

Laurence knew there was a train station in Worcester but he never went there as a young boy. But, during World War II Laurence took the train

Edmond Laurence during World War II, and in a recent photo, at bottom left.

from Union Station to get to his base in Boothbay Harbor in Maine. One time he boarded the train at 3 o'clock in the morning. In those days they referred to the 3 o'clock train as the milk run because it stopped at every station along the way. There were very few commuters at that time of the morning. He would take naps until his train arrived on the beautiful long benches with the contoured backs.

In 1942, Laurence noted that the interior of the station was in fair condition but time had begun to take its toll.

Philip Martin

Bedford, New Hampshire

Thirty-five years have passed since Philip Martin got off the train at Union Station in Worcester, Massachusetts. Why is that significant? Because Martin was the last passenger to disembark the last train in operation at Union Station in 1964.

It marked the end of an era — the end of train travel from our historic Union Station. No more commuters running to catch a train, or children sliding on the shiny oak benches in the waiting room, no more "All Aboard" calls. Martin, then a senior at Worcester Polytechnic Institute in 1964, recalls,

"After my last trip by train, my parents would drive me up from Connecticut. In fact the automobile was by far the most common way to travel back and forth. I do recall being asked a question or two after that last trip, but I don't remember which paper the reporter represented. I was pretty shy with strangers, even at age twenty-one, so I didn't have much to say. I remember wishing that something profound popped into my mind, but it hadn't.

"I can still remember arriving at Worcester Tech for a pre-entry interview three years earlier and thinking Worcester was a big city compared to my home town of Waterford, Connecticut, just outside New London. My first view of the WPI campus sold me — looking up from the main street directly in front of the campus, a street whose name is long gone from my memory thirty-five years later!

Philip Martin as a WPI student, and below, as a grandfather.

"I was an electrical engineering student and found the four years very difficult academically. It seems to me like schools were a lot more rigid then, no co-eds, mandatory classes including ROTC most every Saturday morning (unheard of today).

"I'd characterize my experience as worth the effort but very difficult, even though my grades weren't that bad when all was said and done.

"I used to like to walk to downtown Worcester but generally felt quietly guilty because it always seemed that there was school work which I should be doing — probably because there was."

Yvonne Robichaud LaPointe

Spencer, Massachusetts

Yvonne LaPointe never took the train at Union Station, but she was fascinated by the 1875 photo that her mother-in-law, Gertrude LaPointe was going to throw away. Yvonne salvaged the picture because it looked so interesting, and she put it away for safekeeping.

When all the hoopla about the old Union Station and the present Union Station appeared in the newspapers, LaPointe decided to call and ask me if I would be interested in seeing it. Indeed I was. The photo I had purchased from E.B. Luce was not as clear as the one LaPointe had. I gladly made a copy of it, and it is featured in chapter one. Although the original is credited to E.B. Luce, it is through the courtesy of LaPointe that you see a very clear photo of the old Union Station early on in this book.

CAUGHT IN THE ACT

One Worcester young man confessed that he and his sister would skip school in the 1970's and go to Union Station just because it was so awesome. They were absent from classes so often that the school authorities contacted their father. One morning as they entered the station, there stood their father eye-balling them from the balcony. That was the end of their little escapades.

Ed McMahon

Worcester, Massachusetts

Ed McMahon during World War II.

The Ed McMahon? The one who promises you millions on the sweepstakes commercials? Nope. This Ed McMahon is a former Equipment Installation manager for the New England Telephone Company where he worked for thirty-seven years.

All McMahon remembers about Union Station is the high benches and the Railway Express baggage room. He didn't go there often. When McMahon was drafted during World War II, the war was on the wane, so he wasn't part of the servicemen who traveled from Union Station.

After he retired, McMahon became involved in volunteer work at RSVP (Retired Senior Volunteer Program). He is also a volunteer math teacher at City View School in Worcester. During the summer he teaches a five-week course in various subjects to fifth and sixth graders at the same school. He is also involved in Worcester's Junior Achievement Program, a country-wide organization that encourages youngsters to set goals and work to achieve those goals. McMahon's wife, Claire, is also a dedicated volunteer at City View engaged in reading to children.

On the subject of Union Station, McMahon would like to see a small area in the southwest corner depicting the former Railway Express baggage room. He would also like to see a restaurant (hot dog stand) named Homer's for those who remember Homer's on Front Street, and the benches that were there in the bustling 1940s could be replicated.

"In 1945 Union Station and I were both in pretty good shape." Quipped McMahon. "Now that Union station has been rejuvenated, I too should consider it. A diet and hair transplant would go a long way." McMahon quipped.

Oscar J. Michaud

Worcester, MA

In mid-October of 1934, Michaud recalls that the Depression was in high gear with millions of people unemployed. His brother, Eddy, and Camille Perron, all decided to go to New York City to look for work. Their only means of transportation was by train.

"Arriving at Union Station for the first time remains a beautiful memory," Michaud said. He was awed by the ornate interior walls and tremendously high ceilings. The trio's trip to New York via Springfield took about seven hours. The engine was coal fed. Windows on the train were kept closed to avoid getting soot from the engine's smokestack.

After a few days of work at Bickford's restaurant Michaud opted to hitchhike to the West Coast to look for work and ended up joining the army at Fort Bliss in El Paso, Texas. After serving several months with battery "E" of the 82nd field horse-drawn artillery, he was assigned to serve with Battery "A" on Corregidor in the Philippines.

On or about June 24, 1937, after finishing his tour of military duty, he returned to Worcester. The interior of Union Station was still intact. There appeared to be greater passenger activity than when he left in 1934. Michaud took a taxi to his parent's home on 63 Austin Street.

He returned to Union Station when the United States entered World War II. He was stationed at Fort Devens at the time. Shortly before Christmas, his unit boarded several passenger cars headed for Georgia. Union Station was packed with servicemen. Nearly four years later, after having served in England, Northern Ireland, and Normandy, Michaud returned to Worcester in February, 1945.

On March 3, 1945, he married Louise Frappier. They boarded the train from Union Station bound for New York for their honeymoon.

Oscar J. and Louise Michaud.

Photo by Bryan Mura

A decaying spiral staircase.

Bryan Mura

Auburn, Massachusetts

Union Station 1972

Cold and still,
The faint sound of dripping water
Echoes in the distance.
The wind whistles
Through its empty halls.
Snow covers the once busy benches
In the main hall.
Staring up at the cathedral ceiling–
Decaying plaster reveals steel beams
That resemble the relics of dinosaur bones.
As you stand amidst the empty shell of a building
You can't help imagining
The grandeur of a time gone by.
Train conductors announce departures,
And you hear the subtle roar
Of people rushing to their destinations.
It saddens your heart to see the ruins
Of this once magnificent structure.

Robert W. Mura

Worcester, Massachusetts

Periodically you would hear from different sources that in it's heyday, Union Station was one of the nicest, grandest train stations in the country. You would hear that multitudes of people had fond memories of the bustling station. I remember being in it once with my mother when I was a small child, it was virtually empty then, a rather desolate place as I recall. Years later, I would sometimes have an urge to take a closer look at this once vibrant building.

On a frigid winter day in the early 1970s having just finished a delightful dinner, the winter winds kept at bay by the warmth, camaraderie and laughter of family, my thoughts went to Union Station. On that day, my oldest brother, Bryan and I decided to visit the once majestic, now abandoned train station.

Our unofficial visit, trespassing if you will, began at the rear of the building, at the track level. Descending a set of granite stairs, I stopped my brother about halfway down and told him someone was down there. He wondered how I knew. I told him I could smell cigarette smoke. At this point we had to decide whether it was worth our while to continue, for who were we to encounter at the bottom of this stairway? We both had our reservations about going on, however, after some deliberation, we decided to proceed, hoping that we would not come to regret our decision. We moved to the middle of the stairway, in full alert, hearts pumping, closing in on whatever lay in wait. As we neared the bottom stair and descended into darkness, the cigarette scent growing stronger, we rounded the corner, our eyes adjusting to the darkness.

Scanning the area we spotted the glow of a cigarette in the distance as this was our only way in, we proceeded cautiously. Approaching the glowing cigarette we encountered its possessor, a gentleman who looked youthful in a way, but aged beyond his years, he did not appear to be the menacing type, we nodded politely, may have mumbled a strained greeting and moved on.

He was not the only dweller we were to encounter that day, others were lurking in the shadows. Union Station had become a haven for the homeless.

We noticed someone walking on a balcony high above us, and another stranger was in what appeared to be a boiler room. We were taking pictures here and there and saw a couple of crude beds made with cardboard boxes, newspaper and rags, molded with some cold stranger's imprint.

I could picture someone trying to keep warm there on a bitter cold winter night. We decided it was not wise to linger too long inside and breathed a sigh of relief as we reached the safety of the building's exterior.

Standing amidst the ruins of this cold frozen structure, my memories of that day were ones of sadness, wonder and hope, for how could such a magnificent building fall into such a neglected condition? The building barely had a pulse, "demolition through neglect" as was once written, how lamentable. How fortunate this building was spared the wrecking ball.

John G. Riccio

Worcester, Massachusetts

I first came to Worcester in 1971. I had been hired as a teacher and my assignment brought me to Freeland Street School in the Main South neighborhood of the city. At that time, the area surrounding the school was just beginning to experience the change that seems to come to all long-established neighborhoods in large cities of the industrial northeast.

It was exactly the kind of school for which my degree in urban education had prepared me. This was the chance for me to see if all the theory I had absorbed would really work in a brick and mortar school.

It wasn't long before I felt at home with my fifth grade students and, it seemed, they with me. During the 1973-1974 school year the principal asked me if I would like to work with a student teacher in my classroom. I agreed, never anticipating that the year would bring us so far beyond the walls of the school.

Victor Monroy was an education student at UMASS and needed time in a classroom with a "seasoned" teacher as part of his course of study. From the moment I met him, I knew we were in for a year of surprises. His energy and enthusiasm was surpassed only by his commitment to the students.

As a part of his university studies Victor had to devise a unit of study appropriate to the academic level of the class. After several discussions between us we decided that a study of modes of transportation would offer the necessary connection to the curriculum while at the same time allowing for some exciting activities. Before long, we were planning to take our class and Miss Stanionis's (now Mrs. Decourcey) fourth grade on an excursion to Hartford, Connecticut, via Amtrak.

None of the students had ever been on a train before nor had most of their parents. Usually when teachers recruit parents to act as chaperones on a field trip it is difficult to get the number needed but as plans grew more complete for our train trip we had more parents than we could take. Everyone wanted to "ride the rails." We even had grandparents volunteering to make the trip with us.

After a month of studying about trains in the context of all subjects, reading stories about train travel, solving math problems about time, distance and rate of speed, researching how trains affected the progress of the modern world and examining how steam engines worked and how they differed from diesel fueled engines, we were ready to board the train for Hartford.

As the day approached, the students grew more and more excited. The morning of our departure they arrived at school early, parents in tow, the reverse of what one might see on any other day of school. They had their lunches packed and could not wait to board the bus which was to take us to Union Station in downtown Worcester.

By this time in its' life, Union Station was already a crumbling mass of concrete. It was so dangerous that no one was allowed into the grand waiting hall which had seen so many passengers pass to and from their trains over the years since 1911. Instead, travelers had to make their way through the tunnel on the east side of the building to the boarding area behind. The tunnel was anything but a grand beginning to our day. It was dark and dank and smelled of animals and the homeless transients who used it as a place to sleep and as protection against the elements. Some of the children were frightened as we walked through the tunnel.

Worcester Telegram and Gazette photo.

Cornelius McCarthy, one of the chaperones, with students.

I can remember how cheated we had been that they could not approach our train through the echoes of the waiting room and experience the grandeur of this once magnificent station, one of many between Boston and New York. At the time, many stations along the rails were suffering the same indignities and we could only watch as the national highway system siphoned travelers from the railroads and caused these grand old dames to crumble even more, some to the point beyond repair. Here was another lesson for us to examine when we returned to the classroom after our excursion. After we reached the platform on the other side of the tunnel the children looked through the broken and boarded up windows into the debris-ridden concourse. Their questions about how this all came to be were not easily answered, especially since the adults on the trip couldn't fully understand how such a beautiful monument to a great era of our history could be left to languish as it had.

Our train arrived and we were off to visit the Connecticut Capitol, the offices of the Hartford Courant and the broadcast

Photo courtesy Patricia O'Connor Postales

John Riccio and his class of fifth graders in 1974.

studios of WTIC. We lunched on the lawn behind the capitol building and made our way back to the Hartford railroad station which, unlike Worcester's, had been renovated as an inter-modal transportation center. "Why couldn't they do that in Worcester?" Asked the children. Money? Time? Interest? Vision? We didn't know the answers.

Thankfully, the children of today won't have to ask such questions. Instead, they will have the opportunity to walk through the grand waiting room to the platform and board a train to Boston, New York or even Chicago. They will grow up knowing only the beautiful white station with its twin towers, a center of activity as well as a point of departure and arrival.

No longer will the people of Worcester have to close their eyes as they pass Washington Square or drop their heads when visitors ask what that decrepit old building is. Now that we have our vision back, we can help re-create a masterpiece and leave for our children and grandchildren a treasure which, for some unknown reason, was almost lost to all of us. The following article appeared in the Evening Gazette after our excursion to Hartford.

48 PUPILS RIDE THE RAILS

BY GREGORY R. BYRNES
Of the Gazette Staff

"John get in line!
"Barry, get over here!"
"Andy, where's your group? Hurry up or you'll get lost!"

Yesterday's gathering of 48 youngsters at Union Station, pupils at Freeland Street School looked more like a roundup than a field trip to Hartford, Conn., by way of Penn Central Amtrak train. The youngsters, lined up two by two, were divided into groups of six to eight. They were branded with green tags that gave their

names, home addresses and telephone numbers, destination and departure points. Teachers Barbara Stanionis and John Riccio served as trail bosses. They were assisted by Deborah Menzel, Joanne Caparso and Victor M. Monroy, student teachers, and Mr. and Mrs. Cornelius McCarthy, parents.

It began at 9 a.m. when pupils boarded a school bus for the trip from school to Union Station.

"Woo, Wooooo...." Pupils imitated train sounds as they anxiously awaited the arrival of engine 9532.

"Blow your horn. Blow your horn," shouted the youngsters to the engineer of a freight headed for a Penn Central depot in Framingham.

Deafening yells and screams were let loose when the youngsters finally spotted their westbound train at 10:05. Once aboard, they

A reunion in 1999 at Freeland Street School.

played musical chairs, hopping from one seat to the next and from one car to another.

Several were content to look out giant picture windows as the train whistled through woods and over streams at sixty miles an hour. Others began munching on peanut butter and jelly sandwiches, potato chips and popcorn, and Halloween-size supplies of candy. Some read comic books.

"I like it when the train goes slow," said Donald Ryan, a fourth-grader "I can see everything."

Dana Losaw said she got scared whenever the train went over a bridge. "But I still like it," she said.

"Where's the next bus stop?" asked Andrew Kent.

"Yeah, when do we stop for gas?" chipped in John Ruane.

The questions often stumped Mike Amable, the train's engineer.

A highlight of the ride was a visit to the engineer's room control booth and a tug at the engineer's whistle or "horn" as John Ruane called it. All the youngsters appeared mystified when they didn't see a steering wheel.

After two hours of riding the rails, the pupils arrived in Hartford. They visited the Hartford Courant and radio station WFSB, toured the state capitol and Constitution Plaza, before returning home at 7:30 p.m.

--*Used with permission of The Worcester Telegram and Gazette.*

Judith and Cornelius McCarthy — Chaperones

Judith and Cornelius McCarthy, of Worcester, lucked out when they were chosen to be the chaperones for the memorable trip from Union Station in 1974. Their fond recollections follow.

On April 3, 1974, our family and the students of Freeland Street School, under the direction of teachers, Ms. Barbara (Stanionis) DeCourcey and Mr. John Riccio, had the opportunity to travel by train (Amtrak) destination, Hartford, Ct. For many students, this was their first experience traveling by train. We departed from the historical Union Station in the heart of Worcester. We were fascinated by the architectural foundation and structure of this landmark.

On February 13, 1999, members of the legendary Union Station Field Trip, reunited at our old Alma Mater, Freeland Street School, to kindle old friendships and memories. It was a pleasure to visit with the teachers and staff who originated our unforgettable trip to Hartford, Connecticut It was a special day that the students and adults will cherish forever.

Note: The McCarthy's son, William, was one of the fifth graders who went on the trip and their little daughter Jennifer, went along for the ride also.

Patricia O'Connor Postales

Shrewsbury, Massachusetts

Many years have passed since my fourth grade class trip on an Amtrak train from Union Station in Worcester, Massachusetts. I was only ten years old, but I still remember how excited all the children, parents and teachers were on this big day. Our study of transportation was a valued lesson especially when it included this experience. This was not a usual class trip like going to a museum or a zoo on a bus, but a class trip on a train. A trip - I will never forget.

It seems like only yesterday I was in Mr Riccio's fourth grade class. As we gathered to reminisce about our special trip it was so much fun to see my 4th grade teacher and others such as the parents, Mr. & Mrs. McCarthy who helped chaperone our big day.

Victor Monroy

Holden, Massachusetts

verything started with my student teaching days in the third grade at Freeland Street School in the Spring of 1974, with John Riccio.

I was given the opportunity to develop programs and learning experiences for the study of transportation in social studies. Speakers associated with the railroad, discussions, model trains and such were utilized to prepare the youngsters for their first ride on a train. Some fifty-five people were treated to an exciting trip on Amtrak from Union Station in Worcester, Massachusetts., to Hartford, Connecticut.

After boarding the bus from school to the railroad station, the children anxiously awaited the sound of the whistle, which indicated that the train had arrived. When we heard the shout, "All Aboard," we all hurried into the same car of the train, and we headed for Connecticut.

The happiness and excitement were evident in the children's faces, as we sang songs, ate snacks and traveled rapidly toward our destination. Upon our arrival in Hartford, we visited the State House as well as other sites of interest.

At 5:00 p.m. we boarded the train again for our return to Worcester. Parents were waiting anxiously to hear their children's reactions to their newest adventure. They were most appreciative of those of us who had planned and attended the field trip. Dr. Mullins, school Principal, gave his total support to this venture. A memorable time was had by all. It certainly provided a unique lesson in social studies/career education.

Regarding our recent reunion at the old Freeland Street School, it was wonderful to see one another and have a chance to talk about our lives over the past twenty-four years. How we have all changed!

Ruth (Harrison) Raymus

Cherry Valley, Massachusetts

*W*hen Ruth Raymus was three or four years old she recalls, "My dad used to take my brother Clifton and me to Union Station just to see the trains. Dad was a train buff. He had only one eye so he couldn't become an engineer, but his fascination for trains was always there." Raymus said.

On her first trip to the station when one of the engines let off steam she was so scared she took off, and her dad had to chase after her. She just ran like dickens because she was petrified. Then her dad ran like the dickens to catch her.

Ironically, decades later, when Raymus's husband got called to active duty during the Korean War, Raymus, her dad, along with her two little boys went

to see him off. All of a sudden the train started going and her oldest son ran down the platform and yelled, "I want my Daddy." Again, Raymus's Dad started to run, but this time he was chasing after his grandson, like he'd chased his daughter years before. Her Dad said, "You talk about history repeating itself."

"When I was small, we had relatives who lived in Detroit, Michigan, and we took the train from Union Station to go there. We chose to travel by train because the busses took too long." Raymus said. She remembers Union Station as a huge, huge place, and oh, how she loved those benches. Her brother and she used to slide back and forth on them. She remarks that they were very shiny and they were always immaculate.

Raymus noted that on VJ Day, 1945 (Victory Japan) when she returned from a trip to Detroit, the train was loaded with servicemen.

Mary Scannell

Worcester, Massachusetts

Mary Scannell's first recollection of Union Station is its vast, high ceiling. As a child she remembers the shoe shine boys and she was fascinated by the barbershop. The rest rooms were very nice and the whole station was spotless. On rare occasions Scannell traveled from Union Station with her parents to go to Boston. They didn't own a car, and it was quite an event in those days to go on a trip by train.

The lion sculptures at Christoforo Columbo Park, more commonly known as East Park on Shrewsbury Street in Worcester, are linked with the Scannell family. Scannell's husband's grandfather, Daniel Scannell, worked at a quarry

One of the Griffin statues at East Park.

when the station was built and he is the one who carved the lions for the quarry business. It was never made public that Scannell was the artist who carved the lions, but all their lives the Scannell's family knew that "Old Dan" had designed and carved the lions, yet, there was no way to prove it.

Several years ago Scannell investigated the matter to no avail. Oral tradition has it that Mary Scannell's husband, Joseph E. Scannell's nephew, married a girl whose grandfather told them, "WHEN I WAS A KID, I WATCHED 'OLD DAN' CARVE THOSE LIONS."

An octogenarian, Scannell is treasurer at Bowler's, a wholesale electrical materials business on Green Street, Worcester, a company she and her husband Joseph, (deceased) founded in 1932.

NOTE

*O*ne source claims that the lion sculptures stood guard at the entrance of Worcester's old Union Station in 1875, and another source claims that they were a fixture inside the building. Whatever. Fortunately, they were saved. Another source claims that the lions are the only items left from the old Union Station.

But another artifact exists. The Regulator Clock that adorned the walls of the 1875 station now hangs in the main dining room of Maxwell Silverman's Toolhouse Restaurant in Worcester.

Mari Seder

Worcester, Massachusetts

On special weekends and vacations starting when I turned eight my mother would take me to Union Station and put me on the train to Newton Center. Her instructions to the white-gloved conductor was that Esther Perlmutter would be meeting me at the Newton Center Train Station (now known as Starbucks) and that he should take good care of me.

It was always a treat to visit aunt Esther, my mother's unmarried sister. Aunt Esther was a Phi Beta Kappa graduate of Boston University which didn't impress me at that time. What did impress me, in addition to taking me to movies and Ice Capades, was that Aunt Esther had the biggest collection of books. Aunt Esther was head librarian of the Newton Center Library located right across the street from the train station. The Newton Center Library had a children's reading room with oak chairs, little round tables, some Raggedy Ann dolls and teddy bears; surrounded by stacks of children's books that at the time seemed every bit as grand as the adjacent adult book room.

Many Saturday mornings, especially when it wasn't golf season, my father would go "down" to the Union Station barbershop. It seemed to be a spot for socializing because he would meet many of his friends there. He would come home not only with a haircut and a shave which didn't seem strange, but also with a manicure which to my young stereotypical mind seemed something that only mothers did.

Mari Seder (above) as an eight year-old, and in a recent photo, top right.

Louis Shropshire

Worcester, Massachusetts

Louis Shropshire as a GI during WWII and celebrating his 50th wedding anniversary with wife Chloe.

My childhood recollections of Union Station are of a huge cavernous, bustling place, where bee-hive type activity was taking place in all areas of the building.

I can remember the train announcer mounting his little platform in front of the lighted train board, and calling out in a sonorous voice the arrival of a specific train, its destination, and the stops along its way. I don't know whether he used a microphone or not, or whether the acoustics of the building were particularly good, but his stately measured tones could be clearly heard in every part of that great waiting room.

When I was growing up, it was considered scandalous in my family to go to the movies on Sunday, so, sometimes, my friends and I would go to Union Station, study the train board, and go to the various tracks when trains were due to arrive. We'd wave animatedly at passengers on the express trains as they roared through the terminal, and invariably, we'd get smiles and waves in return. We would wave in a much more subdued fashion to those passengers who were sitting in a stopped train, waiting to disgorge or pick up other passengers.

Even after I became engaged, my fiancée and I would occasionally go to the station and sit on one of the benches at trackside, and lovingly dream of our hoped-for future together. That future of fifty-one glorious years together is now our warmly comforting past. Perhaps in 1999 or later we will again be able to go to the station and hear a mechanically taped recording inform us that train number such and such just left Westboro and is expected in Worcester at such and such a time. It just won't be the same, but then, neither are my wife and I the same.

Shropshire remembers some of the men who worked at Union Station.

There was Raymond Roberts, Bill Perkins, Joe Perkins, Ossie Ford, Sr., and Elwood "Barney" Price, Sr. All of them have checked in their final load of luggage and have found surcease in the eternal Pullman sleeper. Mr. Ford, and Mr. Price left children in the Worcester area, but I think they would have been too young to have retained memories of the building.

After seeing the skeletal steel of the towers on the renovated building Shropshire is withholding judgment on that. His only look was a hurried glimpse as he sped along I-290, but from that glance, he got the impression the framework is far more intricate than he would have favored. It the finished towers are to be so spectacular that they call attention to themselves, they will have defeated their purpose. Rather, Shropshire would have called for straightforward simple lines that would direct the viewers attention to the confident, unadorned beauty of the majestic building.

One item Shropshire has never heard mentioned in any discussion of the old station is the round house. In these days of diesel and electric power, such a building is unnecessary, but when the railroads burned coal for their source of power, the round house or similar facility was a very necessary accouterment. In Worcester, the round house was east of Union Station, somewhere between Shrewsbury and Franklin Streets, under the imposing height of the clock tower that hovered over the bays of the then Railway Express Agency.

"The father of a friend of mine worked at the round house," relates Shropshire, "and one afternoon my friend had to take something to his father. I accompanied him. When we stepped inside I was immediately intimidated by the very large, dirty, ugly presence of the building itself. The glare of powerful, bright, un-shaded bulbs was not enough to disperse the gloom and grime of the accumulated grit and I was happy to escape to the outside air."

The round house was like a gigantic Lazy Susan. The locomotives are towed onto a section of track on a large turntable in the center of the circle. The turntable then revolves to line up with one of the seven or eight other short sections of track and the engine is then unloaded onto one of the short sections. There it will cool, have ashes and cinders removed, and the firebox checked and relined if necessary before it is returned to service.

Elena Simoncini

Worcester, Massachusetts

I met Elena Simoncini at a function at Our Lady of Mount Carmel Recreational Center. Simoncini, age ten, was eager to tell me about her Science Fair exhibit about Union Station at Worcester's Wauwekas Road School.

It was a great opportunity for me to ask her if she'd like to be featured in this book. She was thrilled.

A fifth grade straight "A" student, Simoncini entered her exhibit chronicling important events about Union Station from 1911 to 1999. Her ingenious idea depicting the progress of the station through the years was worthy of the honorable mention she received for her efforts. Simoncini cut out a circle resembling a train wheel with one of the spokes cut out, to show the event and its corresponding year when the wheel is turned. The project took her about eight weeks. Simoncini qualified to show her exhibit (3/26,27,29) in the annual Project Fair held by the Worcester School Department at South High Community

Elena Simoncini with her project on Union Station.

School, where she qualified for a Theme Award for, "How did Union Station Come to Be?"

Simoncini writes: As recently as five years ago, Union Station was a crumbling gloomy structure. Now, Union Station is beautiful to look at. It is most amazing to see every time I go by it how much work has been done. The construction of the new Union Station began in 1995 and is targeted for completion by June of this year. (1999) It is going to cost 64.9 million dollars for the building, which includes a 6.6 million dollar parking garage and 17.8 million dollars to reconstruct the Washington Square rotary in front of the station.

Modern building materials are being used to replicate the original materials and design. They are putting up nine-foot chandeliers and curving staircases to get to the second floor. Also they are putting smoothly polished marble columns. Beautiful elevators with polished brass doors have also been installed. Also stained glass windows have been added to both floors.

I am very proud of what Worcester has done with Union Station. My Mom bought a T-shirt for me at City Hall to help me to celebrate the history of this beautiful building — Union Station.

James Sullivan

Leicester, Massachusetts

ℛ thought Union Station was a large building with an interior that just sparkled when the sun poured through the stained-glass windows. It was like a huge marble auditorium," boasts James Sullivan. Sullivan never took a train from the station as a child; he traveled by trolley car. However, he did have one memorable experience there when he and his friend skipped school and went to the station just to hang around. The truant officer gave them a ride back to school in his old car with a stern warning never to do that again.

Sullivan recalls that in those days the interior of the building was in excellent shape and featured long wooden benches where commuters rested and sometimes managed to stretch out for short naps between legs of a journey.

With the help of his sister, Helen Favreault, they recall that a Thomas Hastings, the ticket seller, was a very busy man at the ticket booth.

As a soldier with the United States Army Transportation Corps during World War II, Sullivan said, "Between furloughs I managed to hit the friendly confines of Worcester's Union Station as often as I could beg, borrow, or steal a pass from my superior officers, which indeed was quite often."

I have no documented proof to offer, but I have always understood that my parents, Patrick Henry Sullivan (born on St. Patrick's day) and my mother (Mary Dolan) were the second couple to depart from Union Station on the day of their wedding in 1911.

Sullivan and his wife, Phyllis boarded the train at Union Station and rode parlor style when they departed for New York City on their honey moon on October 4, 1947.

Phyllis had relatives in and around Boston so she answered the cry of "All Aboard" many times before their marriage and before they purchased their first car, a 1936 Chevrolet in 1948. Sullivan further recalls in the early days of Union Station a gentleman named Alphonse Hebert as the train caller, and for many years Hebert's granddaughter, Bertha Miller, worked the counter.

James and Phyllis Sullivan

Gary Vaillancourt

Sutton, Massachusetts

y father came from a family of nine, and in the late 1950s and early 1960s every Sunday after-noon we would go to my grandparent's house.

As you can imagine, with nine children my grandparents had over thirty-five grandchildren, and on any given Sunday, there were typically twenty people to be fed.

Unlike other families, when the grandmother would cook all day, my grandmother let everyone know that Sunday was her day of rest. Thus, the responsibility of dinner fell to the men in the family. Most people think of take-out as an invention of the 1980s, but the reality was that we had a well established take-out facility even in the 1950s...Water Street in Worcester. My father or uncles would drive into Worcester and pick up bags of fresh bulkies and pimento cream cheese. Nothing ever tasted better and the crowd was always full.

I'll never forget the first time I was considered one of the men and I was allowed to make the trip to the big city...the con-stant hustle and bustle of shoppers on Water Street, the smells, the sights and the taste of the stolen bulkie from the bag, so warm that it would have melted but-ter. As I traveled back home I contin-ued down Water Street until I came to the rotary and the sight of Union Station, a large foreboding building that occupied such a predominant location in the city staggered my mind.

When I asked my father about Union Station he explained that the train station was in fact a major player in his life. It was there that he went off to war and returned, and more impor-tantly it was there that his fiancée met him when he came home from college in Maryland.

I never thought too much about Union Station until I started taking my boys up to Water Street for fresh bulkies. History repeated itself. I guess that is what the grand old lady is all about, tying generations together in just one more way.

Vaillancourt and his wife, Judy, are the owners and propri-etors of Vaillancourt Folk Art, in Sutton, Massachusetts.

Union Station at night before the towers were removed.

Peg Walsh — Worcester, Massachusetts

nion Station has touched many lives with loved ones coming and going. Peg Walsh, Robert Walsh, and Elijah Johnson all agree that Worcester just would not be Worcester without it. A postcard of Union Station at night sent in by Peg Walsh appears above.

95

Cecil Wentzel

Worcester, Massachusetts

Remember dancing on the Starlight Roof of the Bancroft Hotel on Franklin Street to the music of Dol Brissette during the thirties? Remember waltzing to Three O'clock in the Morning, and stepping it up to the Fox Trot, when the band played "Let's Face the Music and Dance?" Remember when couples danced the night away under the hotel's canopied roof? You would if you're a nonagenarian like Wentzel.

These are all pleasant memories for Wentzel. That's where he met his future wife, Lila. (deceased). Wentzel and his wife had two boys an one girl. There are now seven grandchildren, and eight great-grandchildren.

Wentzel's first recollection of Union Station was when he came to Worcester from Intervale, New Hampshire. After leaving the depot he took a street car to his uncle's house at Grant's Square up near Green Hill Park. In the late twenties Wentzel said the interior of Union Station was beautiful. There was a shoe shine parlor, a barbershop, and even a place to eat. He remembers the Hotel Lenox on Front Street, the market, and the pawn shops. He loved to hear the caller announce the trains at Union Station. "All aboard to New York, New Haven, Hartford, Boston and Albany!" Wentzel recalls that there were many commuters during those days. It was a very busy place. He and his wife both loved to visit Union Station on Sunday nights just to watch the trains.

Wentzel grew up in the horse and buggy days. His father was in the carriage business and Wentzel learned the trade from him. He has a unique carriage that he restored displayed proudly in his front yard. A lively ninety-six year old who still drives a car, he is busy at this writing restoring an antique circus horse in his garage.

Madeleine (Brodeur) Westerback

Worcester, Massachusetts

*D*uring World War II Madeleine Brodeur was an American Red Cross Hospital Recreation worker. Her hospital train outfit was moved as a unit from Camp Myles Standish to Fort Lewis, Washington. As their train passed through Worcester, it happened to stop at Union Station. The car in which she was riding stopped directly in front of the window to the Stationmaster's office.

Everyone in the office was leaning out, interested in their unit and its work. Brodeur's family did not know she was on her way to Fort Lewis. She asked if she could phone home to say "so long." One of the secretaries dialed the number, then handed the phone across the platform to the train window. She talked until the high ball signal given. (three whistles). Then the Stationmaster swung his lantern around and around to let the engineer know it was alright to go. It was a happy call for the Brodeur family.

Madeleine Brodeur in front of Union Station. At left, Madeleine sits with members of her family who came to see her off.

David Wright

Auburn, Massachusetts

Like many people, I remember visiting Union Station as a kid. Thinking back, the two most memorable aspects of the station were the cavernous waiting room and the beautiful stained glass ceiling. As I grew older my interests were not with the depot from a public perspective but rather as a control point for the railroad.

The station was built as part of an ambitious program of the New York Central railroad to eliminate all highway crossings at grade from Putnam Lane to Jamesville and westward. As part of the relocation the railroad built tower #26 at the east end of the freight yard and tower #28 at the west end. Tower 26 was a "mechanical interlocking," meaning the operator manipulated the signals and switches under his control with large levers in the tower. Attached were heavy steel rods running from these levers to the various signals and switches. These levers were moved by the sheer physical strength of the operator.

Tower 28 controlled many more signals, switches and train movements than did 26, as tower 28 handled all passenger trains in and out of the station, as well as freight traffic moving east or west and interchanges with the New Haven and Boston and Maine railroads. In the early days of its operation Tower 28 was handling nearly 100 passenger trains a day as well as freight movements. It was a real "hot spot" of railroad activity.

Since this tower controlled so much activity it was built with an interlocking machine consisting of 80 small levers that did their work electrically. It was "state of the art" in 1913, and continued in service until 1966 when the tower was closed and operations controlled remotely from Tower 40 in Springfield.

1966 was my senior year in college. I often visited the tower in the early evenings and talk with the tower-man and watch the operations. When the tower closed I bought the interlocking machine and track model from the railroad for $1.00, and use it as the centerpiece of my own model railroad.

The interlocking machine once used at Union Station and now owned by David Wright.

98

A Fixture on Shrewsbury Street

A book about Union Station would not be complete without mentioning Shrewsbury Street and some of its famous sights. One of the landmarks is Mac's Diner across from East Park.

Mac says that if the lion sculptures across the street could talk they could give you the whole history of Shrewsbury Street.

What Mac remembers about Union Station was shining shoes of sailors and soldiers who packed Union Station in the '40s. They were the best tippers and usually did not need a shine, but they got one anyhow while waiting for their train to come in.

Deedy, a waitress at the diner, says she remembers going to Union Station with her family to welcome her parents friends coming form Brooklyn, N.Y., to spend the summer with them.

The people from New York did not have a park where they lived, and they would just love to vacation all summer because they thought the park was such a beautiful place. Deedy also remembers going to Union Station as a small child with family and friends to welcome service men in her family.

"We'll meet you at the lions," was a popular expression of just about everyone who lived on or around Shrewsbury Street, according to Deedy. She remembers climbing the lions, standing on top of them, and taking pictures in front of them.

John and Ida Evangelista

Worcester, Massachusetts

*A*nother familiar spot on Shrewsbury Street is the Parkway Diner owned by John Evangelista Union Station played a part in John and his wife Ida's marriage. Bottom and top right, John and Ida leaving for their honeymoon from Union Station in 1953. Bottom right, John Evangelista today.

Raymond J. Grimaldo

Worcester, Massachusetts

Raymond Grimaldo, a former shoe shine boy at Union Station is President of Better Electric Company on 190 Grafton Street, Worcester, a business he has owned and operated for fifty years.

The fifth of six children he was born and lived on 3 Wall street growing up. His father died when he was three and his mother died when he was sixteen.

A soft-spoken, personable man, Grimaldo vividly recalls Union Station as the biggest attraction in Worcester in his formative years. At age twelve, Grimaldo quit school to help make ends meet at home. He shined shoes, sold newspapers, as well as doing other odd jobs to earn money.

He made his own shoe shine box from orange crates and started shining shoes on Wall Street and at Union Station. Shoe shine boys, officially known as "BootBlacks," needed a license to operate.

The license cost between twenty-five and fifty cents. The oval-shaped license was held by a large metal safety pin and had to be worn in order to shine shoes. It read: LICENSED BOOTBLACK, Worcester School Committee. 12 age 14, 8306. Name. Raymond Grimaldo, Res. 3 Wall Street, Expires 7/3/43. Conditions: Not to exercise the trade of bootblack without wearing this badge, or in any street where sidewalk traffic is congested or before 6:A.M. or after 8:P.M. Not to have an unlicensed child help you. Not to interfere with the business of others.

Entrepreneur-minded even way back then, Grimaldo bought shoelaces for a penny apiece at a store on Front Street and sold them to customers for five cents. His most lucrative business was on Front Street and Union Station.

"I'll never forget those shoe shine days," Grimaldo says, "they will always be part of my life."

Raymond Grimaldo as a shoe shine boy, and today, at left.

Louis A. Wloch

Spencer, Massachusetts

A little known fact about the Christoforo Columbo monument on the rotary at Washington Square is that a Spencer, Massachusetts man is the Monument Setter who picked up the monument at Mystic Wharf in Chelsea-Boston in 1979. The statue was placed on a GMC tractor 40-foot platform bed using a crane with the help of Wloch's son and a laborer.

Wloch, owner of the Monument Setter business he began in his early twenties speaks with pride about the many monuments in Worcester and surrounding towns that his company has set. The eighteen commemorative benches on the rotary at Washington Square were also set by Wloch.

The Christoforo Columbo monument sculpted by Dino Felici in Italy is a gift to the city of Worcester by Att. Nunziato Fusaro in memory of his wife Esther, who died in 1973. The statue paid homage to the fifteen thousand members of the Italian community in 1979. Appropriately, the statue faces Shrewsbury Street where a large portion of Worcester's Italian population lives.

The inscription on the left base reads:

Not even the mountainous waves of the mighty Atlantic could halt the progress of the Nina, Pinta and Santa Maria under the guidance of the great navigator inspired by the Lord to go forth, search for and find these United States of America.

According to a source at WRA the Christoforo Columbo monument will be moved closer to the station when intersection construction begins.

Wloch, eighty-eight, still works full-time as a maintenance man at St. Joseph's Abbey in Spencer, and he works part-time setting tombstones for Worcester Monument.

His wife Lucille says that she cannot hold him down. He is always on the go. He loves life, and he loves being busy all the time.

The statue of Christopher Columbus gazes towards Shrewsbury Street from Washington Square.

My vision for the future of this facility is a vibrant destination point both for visitors to our fine city and for our residents.

Chapter Seven

The People Behind the Project

James Igoe

Executive Director, Preservation Worcester

*S*imply put, Union Station has been one of Worcester's most important buildings since the city was settled way back in 1722, nearly two hundred and eighty years ago. Sadly, travel habits changed with the growth of automobiles and by the 1960s our station was in serious decline. By the 1970s, it was nearly forgotten and the famous urban renewal folks were saying that it should be demolished. Unfortunately, urban renewal during the 1960s and 1970s only meant demolish the old and build something new. We soon realized that that theory didn't work because too many wonderful and interesting buildings were lost only to be

replaced too often by uninteresting and nonfunctional structures.

Our Union Station was still special to many of the people of Worcester even though it looked pretty shabby, and was considered by some to be structurally unsound and past the point of restoration. Too many people of Worcester remembered the "glory days" of Union Station. They remembered the 1920s and 1930s when train travel was the only way to go. They remembered the 1940s when so many of their loved ones, their fathers, husbands, brothers and sons and daughters went off to defend their country. Many remembered the glorious reunions after years away with their returning heroes.

In 1992, Preservation Worcester asked the city to preserve Union Station "in its entirety" and created a city-wide task force to coordinate the effort to save the building. Preservation Worcester believed that a restored Union Station would be the best intermodal transportation center for the city.

Initially, Preservation Worcester believed that it should be restored just as a train station. Obviously, since the restoration began several years ago, there is now a belief that to be economically successful for the city, the Station must serve additional functions and services.

Completion of the restoration of Union Station will not only preserve one of Worcester's finest treasures, but it will also bring back pride to our people and to our downtown. With its elegant towers and beautiful white terra cotta exterior, Union Station will once again become a beacon to train travelers and a landmark for those who come to revitalized downtown Worcester. We can always build something new but we must use caution and continue to save and preserve the best of the old. Together, the old and the new will provide Worcester with a wonderfully interesting downtown that will bring great success to Worcester in the twenty-first century.

106

A special memory

*C*I remember holding my mother's hand for dear life as we entered the large barrel vaulted hall of Union Station. My parents and I were taking a train to New York City.

I remember that everything appeared larger than life. The main hall was huge. There were people rushing in different directions. There was so much noise — people talking, and loudspeakers announcing arrivals and departures. Then I remember climbing the stairs to the outside platform and viewing the large, hissing train as it awaited us for boarding. I remember the smiling conductor helping my mother and me up the high steps onto the train. It was one of the most exciting adventures of my young life. It happened many years ago, but I'll never forget that morning as a young boy.

James Igoe with his mother and father around the time the family took the train from Union Station for a trip to New York City.

Michael S. Latka

Executive Director, WRA

ichael S. Latka, Executive Director of the Worcester Redevelopment Authority points to crucial funding that enabled Union Station to be transformed.

"The Massachusetts Historical Commission Grant contribution of one-hundred-thousand dollars, and the Federal Funding through ISTEA and its successor Tea-21, had an enormous impact on the progress WRA has made in the renovation of Union Station."

T-21, The Transportation Equity Act for the 21st Century, is the name given to the Federal Legislation (Public Law 105-78) which authorizes Federal highway, highway safety, transit and other surface transportation programs.

Latka continued, "Mention must be made also of the continuous support of the following elected officials: former Congressman Peter Blute went to bat for us early on and Congressman Jim McGovern (Transportation Committee) had a lot of influence, Senator Edward Kennedy and Senator John Kerry were in support the entire time. Credit also goes to Governor William Weld, Governor Paul Cellucci, and State Highway Commissioner Matthew J. Amorello."

Latka also stressed that Preservation Worcester supported the cause. Union Station was put on the Historic Massachusetts' "endangered buildings" list, and Preservation Worcester assisted by lobbying elected leaders to help get Massachusetts Historical and Federal dollars for the project.

The Union Station Alliance helped organize community awareness and support, lobbied elected officials, and assisted with workshops and charities.

The City of Worcester also supported grantsmanship activities to receive State and Federal Funding but no City Funds are allocated to the project, he said.

Julie Sanders

former Project Manager, WRA

Julie Sanders, former Project Manager and architect for the Union Station Restoration Project at WRA (Worcester Redevelopment Authority) since 1993, remembers that during the 1960s only part of the station was open, but the barbershop was still doing business. Charles Podbielsky owned the barber shop for many years. Sanders' husband remembers going there regularly with his grandfather to get his hair cut.

Sanders recalls going to Union Station in the 1970s during the gas crisis. The station was isolated and scary. One had to enter on the barber shop side of the building, then go through a corridor to get to the track side. She boarded the train bound for New York City and returned home by Union Station.

Sanders, a registered architect since 1981, is thankful for the great opportunity to be involved in a very important preservation project — the restoration of Union Station. She has always been interested in historical preservation. A volunteer at Preservation Worcester for several years, Sanders later became President of its Board of Directors.

The Preservation Worcester Organization have been staunch supporters of the restoration of Union Station. They assisted WRA in getting state funds of $150,000 for the restoration project. The Union Station Alliance were the vocal community activist group who pressed for the towers. WRA is working with a number of potential tenants. Restaurants, small businesses, kiosks, and others are in the planning stages. There will be functions for political dignitaries who have been responsible for the project.

Preservation Worcester scheduled a Fund Raiser at the restored Union Station on November 20, 1999. As the station became available, a mayoral inaugural ball was an anticipated event and First Night ceremonies to celebrate the new millennium were also planned..

WRA anticipated rail service to begin about the time this book is published in late 1999. It will be used by AMTRAK and the MBTA, with runs to Boston, Springfield, Chicago, Hartford, and New York. Hopefully, the Providence & Worcester Railroad, now strictly hauling freight, will consider adding passenger service that would run north and south on their lines.

Michael W. Coonan

Business Manager, Plumbers & Pipe fitters Union Local No. 4

Michael W. Coonan, who was recently appointed labor representative on the Worcester Redevelopment Authority by City Manager Thomas R. Hoover, has fond memories of Worcester's Union Station.

"My earliest memories of Union Station are as a child, catching a train with my parents to visit relatives in Pennsylvania. I remember the Hall seemed enormous to me and it was so clean you could have eaten off the floor. As I got older, I remember occasionally hanging out there with friends on the weekends. There was always activity, I recall buying candy and soda from the concessions and sitting on the benches in the Great Hall watching the people come and go. There were barber shops and shoe shine stands and nobody bothered the young people who frequently hung out there. As the years went by, my visits to the station were less frequent and I recall driving by many times as an adult watching this magnificent old building fall further into disrepair.

Reconstruction of Union Station proved to be a slow and careful undertaking. Among other things the craft workers had to maintain and reinforce the structural integrity of the building, recreate architectural details and finishes and at the same time install up to date mechanical and electrical systems. The project was not a real labor intensive one, however, it did prove to be quite a challenge for many of the craftsmen on the job and in many respects a unique project, the likes of which may not be seen in this area for a long time.

My vision for the future of this facility is a vibrant destination point both for visitors to our fine city and also for our residents.

I envision this revitalized jewel as the centerpiece of a redeveloped Washington Square that, when completed, will act as both a link tying together many old and new elements in the city's landscape, and as a catalyst for more development in the Franklin, Winter, and Water Streets area.

The building itself will give many of Worcester's older citizens a look into their past with memories of their ancestors, who came to Worcester through Union Station, or of relatives and friends who went off to war through the Great Hall. To many of Worcester's East side residents it is a sign of a rebirth. The eyesore that they had endured for so long and tried so many times to preserve has finally been reconstructed. The reconstruction is more stunning than many could have imagined.

Union Station has had a long and distinguished history as a focal point of Worcester. It has also survived good times and bad. In this chapter, its history is briefly chronicled in pictures.

Chapter Eight

A Pictorial History of Union Station

Union Station as it was nearing completion in 1911.

E.B. Luce photo

E.B. Luce photo

In 1920, Union Station was in its heyday.

World War I doughboys marching near Union Station.

Men from Webster head for training camp and later for France and World War I.

A car full of men from Southbridge waits at Union Station before heading for Army training camp.

Worcester Historical Museum photo

Crowds salute soldiers marching near Union Station during World War I.

Worcester Historical Museum photo

Patriotism ran deep in Worcester during World War I. Here, an unfurled flag is proudly displayed.

The honored dead return from World War II.

The steel frames of the new towers are outlined against a winter sky.

An architect's concept of the refurbished Union Station.

A sign of the times.

There are those who still follow
ancient rituals which give each worker a
feeling of pride in themselves, such a one
is in construction and performed mainly
by the ironworker — called the topping
out ceremony.

Chapter Nine

Topping Out

A flag and a Christmas tree sit atop one of the iron towers on a gray day in January 1999.

In my quest for material for this book, I did extensive research and dug deep to find items that I had not seen in print. November of 1995 was the first time I spotted a flag and a tree on top of a construction site when the new Gates Lane School was nearing completion.

I was out shooting Worcester buildings when I noticed the American flag and a Christmas tree on top of the building. I wondered what that was all about, and I thought that it must be some kind of tradition. "Some day, I'm going to look into that," I told myself.

Someday happened in January of 1999 when I noticed a similar sight at Worcester's Union Station when the towers were being built.

125

Towers nearing completion.

My research led to dead ends until I called Nancy Gaudette of the Worcester Public Library. Gaudette did not know about the tradition but promised to research it and told me to call her in a week. When I called her, she had tracked down Joseph M. Quilty in Woburn, Massachusetts.

The following article, written by Quilty, explains it all:

The pride of the union worker is not as prevalent now as compared to the days of old. This does not mean that the union worker has lost his or her pride, but because of personal or other problems in this hustle, bustle world, never take the time to remember from whence we came.

There are those who still follow ancient rituals which gives each worker a feeling of pride in themselves, such a one is in construction and performed mainly by the ironworker called, the topping out ceremony; in which a Christmas tree and the flag of our country is placed on a beam, this beam is usually painted white and each ironworker and tradesman signs his name to it before it is erected. This beam is lifted to the highest peak of the building or skyscraper, and is permanently set in place by two ironworkers who are called connectors. As this beam is

Masons at work on the front of the station.

slowly raised, all work on the construction job stops, and for a short time, the pain and hard work have been forgotten and a feeling of pride takes over their whole being. For that moment, he or she is King of the Hill. They have fought the elements of weather and hard work and have won the battle. To each worker this beam belongs to him or her and will remain on the very top of this building as a memorial to those who built it. The history of the Christmas tree is said to go as far

Stairway leading to the balcony.

back as the Norsemen.

As the story goes, the Norsemen venerated the ever-greens — cedars, spruces and pines. The trees were plentiful throughout the frozen reaches of Northern Europe and this provided building materials and firewood for the inhabitants of those wintry regions.

In addition, the evergreens retained their color throughout the year and provided welcome relief from dull hues caused by snow and ice. Those hardy Vikings challenged the seas of Europe and the new world in long

128

ships of seasoned spruce, with tall masts carved from towering pines and steering oars of cedar.

Returning from a particularly successful raid on hapless southern neighbors, Viking chieftains often constructed huge homes — called mead halls. Upon completion these chieftains hoisted an evergreen to the ridge pole in celebration.

So when the topping out beam rises aloft with its customary symbols, the flag and the tree, it offers a link with history. It is a proud link between heroic men of a heroic past and a similar hardy band that also knows what it is to face a challenge and overcome it.

At long last, the architectural beauty that once graced Washington Square has risen from the ashes, manifesting itself before our eyes.

Chapter Ten

Union Station Revisited

Union Station from the eleventh floor of the Bank Boston Building.

On a bright, sunny day in June 1999, I visited Union Station once again to take final photos of the beautifully restored building that barely escaped the wrecking ball. The gleaming terra cotta exterior with its majestic towers reaching heavenward lifted my mood to one of exuberance.

In 1994, when WRA (Worcester Redevelopment Authority) bought the building with plans to restore it and make it useful again, the naysayers were enough to discourage anyone from persisting in their hopes and dreams for the station's future. But WRA held strong, and now after many years of ups and downs, it has been saved through the untiring efforts of WRA, the support of PW (Preservation Worcester), and the continued interest of USA (Union Station Alliance).

I took photos from many vantage points outside; the towers, the lion heads, the canopy frames, the workers toiling diligently to get the job done.

The clock in the main hall.

The interior, although not quit finished, holds great promise. I took photos of the fanlike stained glass windows of the ceiling, the brass trimmed chandeliers, the geometric design of the clock, the winding staircase, etc.

At long last, the architectural beauty that once graced Washington Square has risen from the ashes, manifesting itself before our eyes. The gleaming white terra cotta towers seen from I-290 are a conversation piece. Hopefully, the Intermodal Transportation Center will be a huge success and will once more be Worcester's object of "civic pride" as it was at the turn of the century.

Workers putting the finishing touches on the ceiling windows in the main hall.

At left, a worker lays the tile floor above the main hall.

Above: three workers take a coffee break outside the station.

At right, a closeup shows the ornate detail of the left tower.

Above: A refurbished lion growls silently as he overlooks Washington Square.

At left, a lamp pedestal commemorates the completion of the Union Station project.

Above: the passenger platform.

A view of Union Station from Grafton Street.

Through the trees from the El Morocco parking lot.

From the park at Washington Square.

From the Author

*T*he more people I interviewed for this book, the more I was fascinated by their interesting stories, and soon the whole project became my passion. I kept finding subjects to write about right up to the week before the book went to press. I wrote until all hours of the night, and then I processed photos to give *Union Station: The Monument and the Memories* the special visual appeal that my publisher and I wanted the book to have.

I must admit, however, that initially I did not have a book in mind. It all began as a photography project at the Worcester Center for Crafts in 1994 and evolved into this book during the next five years.

When our photography instructor, Peter Faulkner, suggested that we apply for grants to exhibit our work, I came up with a title for my exhibit — *State of the Union* — even before I applied for the grant! With a title like that, I just knew there was something bigger in the wings, but I had no idea what that something was.

I received a grant from the Worcester Cultural Commission, and my first exhibit, a photo essay at the Worcester Center for Crafts, featured forty photos of Union Station from 1911 to 1995. The subject matter struck a community chord and attracted more than two hundred people. Further exhibits of fifty-two photos were shown at the Rose Madder Gallery, UMASS Medical, and the Worcester Public Library.

At some point, it became clear to me that both the city and I were ready for a book on Union Station.

About the Author

Photo by Chris Christo
Worcester Telegram & Gazette.

Idamay Michaud Arsenault was born in Maine and moved to Worcester, Massachusetts as a young girl. She has been in love with the city ever since.

She began her professional writing career in 1965. In 1979, she became interested in photography which soon became her passion. Her photographs have won awards from the Worcester Science Center, the Audubon Society, and Worcester State College.

Her passion for photography led her to chronicle the rise, fall, and rebirth of Union Station.

All uncredited photographs of Union Station were taken by Ms. Arsenault.

Her work has been exhibited numerous times. At the time of publication, many of her Union Station photographs were on exhibit at Preservation Worcester and at the refurbished Union Station.

Idamay and her husband, Jerry, live in Worcester.